D1798713

"PIE-POWDER"

"PIE-POWDER"

BEING

DUST FROM THE LAW COURTS

COLLECTED AND RECOLLECTED
ON
THE WESTERN CIRCUIT

BY A CIRCUIT TRAMP

(J. ALDERSON FOOTE)

EP
PUBLISHING LIMITED
1973

Copyright © 1973 EP Publishing Limited
East Ardsley, Wakefield
Yorkshire, England

First published John Murray, London 1911

Original book kindly loaned by
East Sussex County Library

ISBN 0 85409 878 x

Please address all enquiries to EP Publishing Ltd.
(address as above)

Printed in Great Britain by
The Scolar Press Limited, Menston, Yorkshire

CONTENTS

CHAPTER I
CIRCUIT

CHAPTER II
THE WESTERN CIRCUIT

CHAPTER III
SESSIONS

CHAPTER IV
THE CIVIL COURT

CHAPTER V
THE CRIMINAL COURT

CHAPTER VI
ADVOCACY

CHAPTER VII
ON EVIDENCE

"PIE-POWDER"

Circitor haec scripsi, paganas dicere causas
   Doctus, et incultis promere jura locis.
Talia versanti mihi provenere quot anni!
   Pulveris o quantum! quantus et aestus erat!
Quod si canities nugarum offenderit usquam,
   Ecce viae crimen, pulvereique pedis!

"PIE-POWDER"

CHAPTER I

CIRCUIT

THE reminiscences of so many eminent lawyers have been written, either by themselves or by those who were once their friends, that it has occurred to a mere Circuit Tramp to try the experiment of recording what he remembers of a circuit and a profession, rather than the history of a professor or a circuiteer. In truth that which men remember about themselves is generally that which others are most willing to forget; and the autobiographer would give most pleasure who could set down on paper his friends' recollections of him in place of his own. For this reason autobiography has become for the most part a sacrificial offering to posterity rather than a commemoration of realities; and he who would perform this

B

sacrifice with the most grace must do it at the altar of his self-respect.

But although men remember little worthy of mention concerning themselves, there are few so unobservant as to pass through life without noticing much that was memorable in others. As the years pass by the storehouse of memory becomes more crowded, until the time comes when we forget more quickly than we acquire, and recollection loses more at one end of the chain than it gains at the other. I am myself conscious of having forgotten so much that once seemed worth remembrance, that the task of setting the residue down on paper must be commenced at once, if it is to be attempted at all. The critic will perhaps be provoked to say, that no poorer excuse can be offered.

It is impossible that the record of such personal reminiscences as these should be without a certain flavour of egotism, and perhaps even some colour of conceit. Without concealing these essential qualities altogether, the writer will endeavour to drape them modestly from the public view. The reader shall be spared the details of the birth, parentage, and education of the chronicler. His religious and philosophical views, or those ideas which appear to him as such, shall be carefully concealed; nor shall the pages of his fee-book be indecently exposed. The confidences of friendship shall not be violated, except where he believes that friendship would condone the offence; and although to speak well of all men would be monotonous, even if it were possible, he will endeavour to speak more or less truly of some, without either passing censure or provoking it. And being conscious that the attitude of a timid and shivering bather does not always commend itself to the spectators, let him take the plunge at once, even if he tumble in backwards.

.   .   .   .   .   .

The Justices in Eyre and Commissioners of Assize have gone circuit for so many years that each successive generation of lawyers is justified in believing that the system will outlive its critics. The legal reformer has waged war upon it, at any rate for the last thirty or forty years, but hitherto without complete success. That much of its glory has departed is incontestable. There was a time, and that long after the enervating effects of railway development had made themselves felt, when the common-law barrister who did not go circuit was a rare phenomenon. The practitioners in the Ecclesiastical Courts and in Admiralty were no doubt exceptions, and there were a few criminal advocates who devoted themselves mainly to the metropolis ; but the great majority of the profession looked to circuit as the mainstay of their livelihood, and certainly as the surest road to professional success. Two judges visited each assize town twice a year, and the common-law courts in London were closed, as they had been for centuries, for six weeks, while Justice toured in the provinces. The Home Circuit was a reality ; the Northern was a great power ; the Western, the Oxford, and the Midland had not begun to decay. The change that has crept over them has been gradual, but its magnitude cannot be ignored ; and before I speak of the circuit which I know best, it may be useful to enumerate very briefly the causes which have been at work to cause the decadence of all.

First and most important, in my judgment, has been the enormous progress which has been made during the last fifty years in travelling by railway. The assize towns which are situated within fifty or sixty miles of London have become for business purposes parts of the metropolitan system. Croydon, Guildford, Maidstone, Lewes, Chelmsford, Hertford, Bedford, for example, have largely lost their provincial character. Solicitors, litigants, and witnesses can run up to town in time for the sitting of the courts, and return to their homes by dinner-time. Barristers, of course, can make the reverse journey with the same facility, and when they go to these places at all, they dine and sleep in Kensington and Bayswater. The more distant towns are affected in the same manner, though perhaps to a less extent. When York and Exeter were two days' journey from London, it would have been a denial of justice to have compelled litigants to come to the metropolis. Sixty years ago, Macaulay noted almost with awe that travellers were whirled to London from these provincial centres "by the light of a single winter's day." In our own time we have seen the duration of such a journey diminished by more than a half. The provincial solicitor who consults his own inclination enters his causes in the Middlesex lists whenever he can

B 2

do so, and naturally finds the Strand more attractive than the Assize Court of his native town. It is, moreover, an undoubted fact that juries give larger damages in London than they do in the provinces; and I remember a client who was deprived of costs by Sir Henry Hawkins on the ground that the cause ought to have been tried in Dorsetshire, but who consoled himself by the reflection that he had recovered five hundred pounds where a country jury would have given him fifty. The importance of the assize town has in fact dwindled from the same causes which have dimmed the social glories of provincial capitals like Norwich and York. The iron rail has been the surest instrument of centralization.

The second powerful agency which has done so much to destroy the prestige of circuit is, of course, the creation and extended jurisdiction of the County Courts, coupled with the improvements in procedure by which judgment can be obtained in practically un-defended cases without the delay of going to trial. I doubt whether the effect of "Order XIV" upon the circuit cause-lists has ever been properly appreciated. Fifty years ago any defendant who was desirous

of putting off the evil day could offer a
passive resistance to the plaintiff until the
time came for the cause to be heard in court.
It is true that the defendant who is willing
to swear to an unreal defence can still do so,
and very often does. There are, however,
a great many cases in which the defendant
declines to perjure himself, probably not from
any conscientious scruple, but because the
documents and facts render it impossible for
him to do so plausibly. There is a still
larger number in which the necessary perjury
is committed, but is not believed. None of
these cases come into the lists for trial as
they did formerly. At many assize towns
there would be scores of undefended cases,
which were usually taken first, and were in
some places regarded as a sort of perquisite
of the senior leader of the circuit. The effect
of the County Court upon the assizes varies
very much in different localities. But in
districts where the County Court judge com-
mands the confidence of the public—as he
frequently but not invariably does—many
cases involving important rights are tried
before him which would naturally have been
brought in the High Court, or removed to

it, if the County Court judge had been less popular. One of the practical objections to the suggested fusion of the County Courts and High Court is, that under any system which allowed the litigants the option of choosing their tribunal some of the County Courts would be deserted and others swamped. There are other objections, of course, but this is not the place to discuss them.

There is a third cause which has operated —perhaps more than any other—to diminish the prestige and importance of the circuits. The institution of continuous legal sittings in London, and the strenuous efforts which have been made to maintain them, have gravely affected the Bar as a profession. Speaking generally, the common-law Bar may now be divided into two groups — the men who habitually go circuit, and the men who prac tise almost exclusively in the metropolis. The London work is naturally the most attractive and the most important, and it may very probably be for the public benefit that the best advocates of the day should devote themselves to it, and should decline to hold briefs at the assizes except at prohibitive fees ; but the fact that they do so is undeniable.

It is also certain that this distinction did not formerly exist. It has been the natural consequence of alterations which have not only created the competition between the London sittings and the assizes, but have intensified it by prolonging the duration of the latter under the one-judge system. The addition of a third assize in the year, and in some places even a fourth, has added to the difficulty. The effect upon the Bar has been very considerable. Thirty or forty years ago the leaders of the chief circuits were also the leaders of the metropolitan common-law Bar ; an assertion which is sufficiently proved by the mere enumeration of such names as Coleridge, Day, Karslake, Huddleston, Henry James, Hardinge Giffard, and Henry Matthews.

At the present day things are very different. The fashionable advocates of the hour may retain their names on the circuit lists, but they are seldom indeed seen at assizes. Such a state of things necessarily reacts upon the civil business. It is notorious that nothing is worse for a circuit, from a material point of view, than a deficiency, or supposed deficiency, of efficient leaders. Litigants will not try their cases unless they believe that they command the services of advocates of the first rank. It is sufficient if they believe this, and whether they believe it rightly or wrongly is quite immaterial; but unless the belief is there the cause-lists will inevitably shrink. Nor is the evil much abated when the juniors on a circuit become busier and better than the leaders; which happens sometimes, though it has never yet been suspected, except by their clerks.

Enough has been said—probably too much —to explain the reasons why the ancient glory of Circuit has somewhat waned. It is tolerably certain that in one form or another provincial sittings of the High Court of Justice will always be demanded by the country. That some new names will be found for them is very possible. The present nomenclature is too picturesque for an age which has instituted a Bar Council, which has abolished the coif and rings of Serjeants' Inn, and which has already forgotten the Barons, the Tubman, and the Postman of the Court of Exchequer. Under some more utilitarian label, however, I do not doubt that circuits will in substance still endure; and it may be that a younger generation of advocates may

find some interest in the desultory reminiscences of a circuit which has been as distinguished as any, and which has preserved
more studiously than some the spirit and
tradition of a great past.   So, at least, those
who still tread its dusty paths may be permitted to believe.

.   .   .   .   .   .

In truth it is a goodly land and fair, through
which His Majesty's judges follow those
well-worn ways.   Fairest, without doubt, in
summer, when the southward uplands are
bathed in sunshine, and the lanes are starred
with wild roses and guarded by nodding fox-
glove ; but still fair in misty autumn or chilly
winter, with the solemn beauty of time-worn
stones and everlasting hills.   First in order rises
before the eye the spire of Salisbury, that cuts
the sky as surely no other pinnacle ever raised
by man ; and few there are who have not
leisure there to wander out to the desolation
of Old Sarum, to view in imagination the
ancient cathedral and monkish houses that
were crowded once within those grassy slopes.
If any man doubt the tale, let him visit the
cathedral close of the modern city.   Built

into the great wall that bounds it on the east
he shall find the very stones of Old Sarum itself, carved fragments of decorated arch and
column, that were brought there by the thrifty
monks who moved the shrine seven hundred
years ago.   If time permit, but half a score of
miles and the wanderer may stand before the
altar of Stonehenge, that mighty mystery in
stone that baffles philosopher and historian
alike.   Older still are the stones of Avebury,
and he may reach them too—more easily in
winter, when the circuit goes to sleepy Devizes,
on the other side of Salisbury Plain.   What
god was worshipped there we know not, but
surely men must have prayed even then in the
words of Isaiah, saying, " Doubtless thou art
our father."

The sheriff's trumpeters blow next at Dorchester, where the judge's rooms stand almost
opposite the ancient house where Jeffreys
lodged at his first stage on the Bloody Assize
of evil fame.   The wandering junior there may
feel a pang of envy, when he thinks of the
plenteous store of Treasury briefs that must
have been distributed in that dreadful year.
He will console himself, if he is wise, by visit-
ing the huge ramparts of chalk that sheltered

the British tribes against the legions of Rome, the circus where the conquerors sat to watch the chariots file in at the gateway which can still be distinguished, and the Roman roads that run straight and far over the Wessex hills, cutting across the tracks and driftways of an earlier age. It was on these bare uplands that the population crowded most thickly in those primeval days, when the greater part of the land was impenetrable forest or impassable morass ; and men have left their footsteps plainer there than on the alluvial midland plains or the bleaker hills of the north. The granite moors of Devon and Cornwall are in like fashion studded thickly with hut-circles, avenues, and cromlechs—the relics of a still older race.

The circuit wanderer passes on to the pleasant vale of Taunton ; and in summer to the graceful fane of Wells, with its richly decorated front. At the very door of the Assize Court lies the cathedral close, fringed with low stone buildings of immemorial age, and carpeted with green turf that must surely be as old as they. He may pass his time, until his solitary case comes on, beneath the cool shadows of the elms that guard the palace moat; or he may cross the greensward, and find what seems like a fragment of an Oxford college hidden behind the deanery walls. If the court rises early, an hour's drive will take him to the cliffs and caves of Cheddar, and he may climb the gorge to the summit of the Mendip range. On the other side of Wells, within a couple of hours' walk, stand the ruins of holy Glastonbury, and Glastonbury Tor itself, even more sacred to the devout as the legendary birthplace of the English Church. There he may take his midday meal at the oldest inn in England, within two miles of the oldest human habitations in Europe—the lake-dwellings of the Somersetshire fens. In the blue distance lie the flats of Sedgemoor, whence Monmouth fled, mudstained and inglorious, from the last battlefield on English soil. All this he may see, and more, who follows the circuit to Avilion's sunny isle.

Cornwall comes next in order, and the bleak Bodmin moors, with the long street of the little town stretching up the hill on the old coach road to "Indian Queen," Truro, and Penzance. Thence on Saturday afternoon—perhaps even on Sunday—the sheriff will drive the judge northward to wild Tintagel, where

King Arthur's castle still endures the buffet-
ings of Atlantic gales. Or southward to
Fowey, beloved of yachtsmen, where the sea
seems always to smile, and the hills of the
little harbour are always green. And if there
be any with time enough, before the opening
of the commission at Exeter, to travel back
by road across the Cornish moors, they will
pass over Brown Willy, from whose summit,
on a clear day, they may perchance discern
the two seas that wash the peninsula of the
West.

By road or by rail—and some adventurous
spirits have even gone by sea—the circuit
passes on to Exeter, the Ever-Faithful City,
set in the midst of the garden of England.
The noisy trams have of late profaned that
ancient and beautiful street ; and the old stone
bridge across the Exe—the gateway to Dart-
moor and the West—has given place to con-
crete and iron. But still we walk beneath the
elms of Northernhay, where the rooks caw
above the red ruins of Rougemont, and bow
our heads in the mighty nave of St. Peter,
conscious of the abiding presence of the Past,
and remembering the generations of men.
Macaulay writes that two hundred years ago

York, Norwich, and Exeter were the most typical and important of English provincial towns. Their supremacy has long since passed away, and the great industrial hives of the north have usurped their rank; but the old cathedral city of the west, with the names of over seven hundred mayors on its roll, is still as little comparable to Manchester as it is to Chicago.

Eastward to Winchester next, and William of Wykeham's long nave, with the legendary table of King Arthur in the Castle Hall, and King Alfred's statue guarding the High Street below. Here, when the assizes fell after the older fashion in late July, we of the Bar were wont to meet after mess beneath the lime trees in the quiet close—less spacious than Salisbury, less green, perhaps, than Wells, but with greater memories, as befits an ancient capital of the realm. At Winchester we need not look over-anxiously for briefs, so long as it is given to us to watch the school eleven at cricket, to count the trout in the clear chalk stream beneath the bridges, to climb to the ancient camp on St. Catherine's Hill, and so back by fair St. Cross in time for circuit mess. Here too it has long been the custom for the

Bar to dine with the judges in solemn form, and to drink with them, amongst other time-honoured toasts, " Prosperity to the Western Circuit ! " The days have gone by when " Cras Animarum " was the last and farewell toast at the summer assizes—meaningless, alas ! now that the long vacation has been touched by sacrilegious hands, and the courts meet again perforce in October, long before the dawn of the morrow of All Souls.

Last of all to Bristol, where tall masts and salt-washed funnels still rise in the midst of a modern city—a city of docks and churches, of factories and tramways, of ancient arch-ways and climbing steps, all thrown together by the careless hand of time. At Bristol there should be briefs, and sometimes are ; but of banqueting and feasting there is never any lack, Lord Mayor and Sheriff vying with each other in indiscriminate and genial hos-pitality to all. The cathedral on College Green may not, in truth, be compared with the towers of Exeter or the spire of Salis-bury ; yet the great Norman archway that leads to the chapter-house makes amends for much, and men may seek far and wide with-out finding a nobler pile than the church of

c

St. Mary Redcliffe, where the ill-fated Chatterton dreamed his short poetic life. And when after the day's labours we climb to the downs, above the gorge of St. Vincent's Rocks, we may watch the sun set behind the Somersetshire hills, or look northward to the blue coast of Wales; whilst three hundred feet beneath us, great ships go on the tide of Avon to the sea.

THE COUNTRY OF THE WEST

The wind blows sweet on Surrey hills among the pine trees' crests,
Across the Weald the Sussex downs uplift their stately breasts,
The Southern Coast makes holiday for many a merry mile,
And from the Thames to Dover Cliff the Kentish orchards smile;
But there's a fairer land that lies towards the setting sun,
A land where lovers wander, and singing waters run;
There first I met Life's sunshine, there would I fain find rest,
In that enchanted country—the Country of the West!

Through water meads the Itchen glides, the Test flows smooth and cool,
With grayling on the shallows, and trout in every pool;
Full many a lusty pike there lies in Avon's sedgy deeps,
And by the Christchurch meadows oft the silver salmon leaps;

But faster runs the amber Teign, that goes by Chag-
ford Mill

To Fingle Bridge, in shadow hid beneath its folded hill,

By Christow banks and Chudleigh town—a smiling
countryside—

And slips between the golden sands to meet the Shal-
don tide.

O ruddy cliffs and opal seas! O sunny shore and blest!

That lies beneath the headlands, in the Country of the
West!

The Wiltshire downs stretch wide and free around the
Sacred Stones,

With many an ancient mound and cairn that covers
dead men's bones;

On Quantock Hills the red deer roams, the Mendips
hide their caves,

And Lynton Rocks rise steep and stark above the
Severn waves;

But O! the Spirit of the Moor calls with a mightier force

To clattered tor and shaking peat, the granite and the
gorse;

Where in the spring the yellow bloom sets all the hill
on fire,

And Dart and Taw and Tavy rise from out the lonely
mire;

Downward by coombe and cleave they run, like children
out of school,

They chatter on the stickle, they slumber in the pool,

They loiter by the stepping-stones, they linger at the fen,

Until by hamlet and by town they come to homes of men.

O kindly folk and pleasant homes! the land that I love
best,

The moor and vale of Devon, in the Country of the
West!

CHAPTER II

THE WESTERN CIRCUIT

THE Western Circuit, when the writer's long association with it commenced, had barely emerged from the limelight of its greatest glories. Coleridge and Karslake had only just ceased to be its leaders; Cockburn was remembered by most; Collier, Erle, and Montague Smith were still familiar names at the mess-table; and Bowen, though still a member of the circuit, was in fact withdrawn from it by his more engrossing duties as Attorney-General's devil. The natural consequence of such a retrospect was that all its active members were sanguine as to their own prospects of like distinction. The wholly inexperienced, who joined in the year of which I write, were more than sanguine—they were convinced. We had some uncertainty in our own minds as to which of our group was to be Lord Chief Justice first, and which was fated to rise to no higher office than that of

Attorney-General ; but that all of us were qualified, and most of us destined by Fortune, for judicial rank, we had no doubt whatever. Those who still survive are accustomed to console themselves by the reflection that these things largely depend upon chance. The present Lord Chancellor recently gave his sanction to this comforting doctrine—I think in an after-dinner speech ; and a truth which is endorsed by the modesty of success may be adopted without injury to the self-esteem of any. It is, after all, much harder to become a poor philosopher than a good judge, though it may be easier to be dignified upon the bench than in a tub.

The working leaders of the circuit, when the writer joined the mess at Dorchester between thirty and forty years ago, were H. T. Cole and Henry Lopes. The latter became better known as a Lord Justice of Appeal, and eventually as Lord Ludlow. Cole was the elder of the two, and then sat as Liberal member for a Cornish constituency— the Penryn boroughs. He was essentially a common-jury advocate of the old-fashioned school—perhaps "rough-and-tumble" would be a more descriptive epithet. Lopes was equally resolute in his methods, though belonging to a different class; and unfortunately the two were not always on the best of terms. Not to put too fine a point upon it, they disliked each other cordially; and quarrelled almost without cessation, both in ·court and out of it. It is not the custom for the leading advocates of the present day to quarrel, except occasionally with the judge—or during the luncheon interval; but it has not always been so; and things have been said in public, even by men of acknowledged position, which appear almost incredible when written down. I remember, for example, a Board of Trade inquiry, where the leader on one side interrupted his opponent by declaring that his nerves would not allow him to remain in court, unless his learned friend moderated "his strident voice." The strident one retorted that he would endeavour to do so, if his learned friend would "turn away his ugly face"! Both criticisms were perfectly just. It is true that these were leaders of the Parliamentary Bar; and I do not suggest that Cole and Lopes, or any other circuit leaders, ever went to similar lengths. Still, there was considerable friction between them, on which they greatly flourished ; and Cole was never quite the same man after Lopes left the circuit for the Bench. He had not had a classical education ; and almost the first case in which I remember his oratory was one in which he had to explain to a jury how parasites known as " flukes " are developed in the livers of sheep. There was an audible shudder in court when the junior Bar heard the " *ovums* of these little creatures " referred to. " I hear my young friends laughing at me," said Cole, dimly conscious of something wrong. " They have been at school since I have—but of course I know that, strictly speaking, *ovums* should be *ovæ.*"

The other Queen's Counsel on the circuit at this time were T. K. Kingdon and C. G. Prideaux. Kingdon was a learned real-property lawyer ; Prideaux had written a book about churchwardens, and was popularly supposed to know Shakespeare by heart. It is pleasant to add that these qualifications obtained for each of them in turn the substantial emoluments of the Recordership of Bristol.

Passing from leaders to juniors, the most conspicuous men on the circuit at the date of which I write were Arthur Charles and

F. F. Pinder—another learned lawyer of the older school, who died suddenly just as he had sent in his application for silk. It is not an exaggeration to say that in four causes out of five these two appeared as juniors to Lopes and Cole. Certainly the work was far less widely distributed at that time than in more recent years. The great lawyer afterwards known as Lord Bowen was nominally still a member of the circuit; but he was then junior counsel to the Treasury, having been appointed to that office by Sir John Coleridge two or three years before. The Attorney-General's "devil" is of course practically compelled to give up circuit, but I remember Bowen appearing at Winchester as junior in a big cause about a right-of-way over the pier at Cowes. Visitors to the Isle of Wight can still see a seven-foot path from the gangway to the shore, which represents the result to the public of that litigation. I do not think Bowen's practice on circuit had ever been large; but to describe in these desultory pages his reputation as a lawyer, a wit, and a companion would be impossible. For a short time only he served as a puisne judge, and was then promoted to the Court of

Appeal, which never sustained a greater loss than by his premature death. There was an academic refinement about his humour, a delicacy in his sarcasm, and a kindliness in his wit which made his after-dinner speeches as brilliant as his judgments in the Court of Appeal. Unfortunately, most of his epigrams are so well known, that one almost hesitates to repeat them here, except for the benefit of non-professional readers. The most classical example is his emendation of the address presented to the Queen by the judges on the occasion of the opening of the new Law Courts in the Strand. One of the paragraphs of this address commenced " Conscious as we are of our own shortcomings," and when the draft was being settled, one of the judges objected to this on the obvious ground that it was hypocritical. " That objection can easily be met," said Bowen suavely. " May I suggest that ' Conscious as we are of each other's shortcomings ' will read much better ! " The hypocrites had their way, however ; as a reference to L.R. 10 Q.B.D. 3 will sufficiently establish. Another famous example, which the present writer was fortunate enough to hear personally, was addressed to a barrister

arguing a bad point in the Court of Appeal
on the ground of an "equity" in the case.
"When I hear of an 'equity' in a case like
this," Bowen said with judicial gravity, "I am
reminded of a blind man—in a dark room—
looking for a black hat—which isn't there!"
Within the last few months I have seen this
misquoted in the press as a search for a 'black
cat'—a variation which I feel assured that the
late Lord Justice would have strongly dis-
approved.

One more judicial utterance, often attributed to Lord Justice Mathew, and sometimes even to Mr. Justice Maule, was really
crystallized by Bowen—I mean the famous
dictum that "Truth will leak out—even in an
affidavit!" It has been recently demonstrated
by a writer in the press that this was an adap-
tation from a phrase used by Charles Reade
in *The Cloister and the Hearth;* but Bowen
was certainly the sculptor who gave it artistic
merit, even if he had ever seen it in the novel
—which I greatly doubt. The form in which
the novelist presented his idea conveys, indeed, a different intention to the mind. "He
had spoken the Truth! And in an AFFIDA-
VIT!!!" is the version presented by Charles

Reade, which borrows most of its point from italics, capital letters, and meretricious notes of admiration.

Of Bowen's after-dinner stories, the best is probably that which I heard him deliver when Mr. Justice Charles was entertained by old and present members of the circuit on his elevation to the Bench. Every post-prandial orator has borrowed it since; but in its original form, and delivered with Bowen's characteristic voice and manner, it was inimitable. " One of the ancient Rabbinical writers —I have forgotten his name, but I have no doubt that it can be easily ascertained—was engaged in compiling a history of the minor prophets ; and in due course it became his duty to record the history of the prophet Daniel. In speaking of the most striking incident in that great man's career — I refer to his critical position in the den of lions—he made a remark which has always appeared to me replete with judgment and observation. He said that the prophet, notwithstanding the trying circumstances in which he was placed, had one consolation which has sometimes been forgotten. He had the consolation of knowing, that when the dreadful banquet was over, at any rate it was not he who would be called upon to return thanks!" Another scriptural story has been attributed to Bowen of a theological student endeavouring to pass a *vivâ voce* examination before an episcopal chaplain. "What can you tell me about Titus?" asked the examiner. "He was one of the later Roman emperors," responded the candidate nervously, "and—and he wrote an epistle to the Ephesians." "Anything more?" said the questioner, raising his eyelids. The student hesitated a moment, and then in desperation completed the biography. "His other name was Oates!"

Besides the juniors who have been mentioned, there were others whose names were or afterwards became well known. The present Mr. Justice Bucknill was practising at the Devon sessions, and I remember Arthur Charles pointing him out as one who would some day lead the circuit. Sir Walter Phillimore did not join the Western till a much later date, when he was elected as a mark of special grace by the circuit mess long after the period of limitation. The most conspicuous personality of all, however,

both then and for many years afterwards, was
Edward Bullen. It was, I think, the infectious
gaiety of his temperament and the genial
assurance of his demeanour, rather than
eloquence or even wit, that earned the
enormous popularity he so long enjoyed.
He had the happy knack not only of reduc-
ing a hostile witness to insignificance, but
even of overwhelming his opponent with
banter rather than bluster. " Don't answer
me, sir ! " he has been heard to exclaim to a
victim under cross-examination ; and a broad
smile would spread over the jury-box, extend-
ing sometimes as far as the Bench itself. None
the less, he was an admirable lawyer ; and retained to the day of his death an hereditary
instinct for that special pleading which has
now become a lost art. He could vivify even
the dry bones of a defence under the Judicature Act. The gravity of the Court of
Appeal was once seriously disturbed by his
rea   ₒ to them the following paragraph from
a pleading in an action for seduction : "The
defendant denies that he is the father of the
said twins, *or of either of them.*" This, he
apologetically explained, was due to an accident in his pupil-room ; but every one recog-

nized the style of the master-hand. In the
same spirit, when a judge at Nisi Prius com-
mented on the order in which he called his
witnesses, saying that he thought he had
called his best man first, " Hardly my best
man, my lord," responded Bullen; with blush-
ing modesty. " He gave me away ! " It was
probably due to pure laziness that he never
took silk, and so missed the eminence he
might easily have attained.

Of the others who were then stuff gowns-
men, the names of Arthur Collins (afterwards
Chief Justice of Madras), Petheram (Chief
Justice of the North-Western Provinces),
and Norris (who became a puisne judge in
Calcutta) are a trio naturally grouped by
their common destiny. J. C. Norris was
perhaps the most memorable, and certainly
the most eccentric of the three. He had
been better known in the Western Counties
than in London ; but became famous, almost
as soon as he landed in India, by holding
thirteen trumps in his own hand when play-
ing whist at the Calcutta Club. I need not
say that this was before the days of bridge.
The *Field* devoted several columns to showing that, according to the ordinary laws of

probability, such a phenomenon could not have been reasonably expected, even if the whole world had done nothing but play whist since the Creation; and one correspondent remarked that it was fortunate that the miracle had happened to one so entirely above suspicion as a High Court judge. Norris soon afterwards acquired additional renown by his punctilious adherence to the laws of evidence, in a case of great importance to the native community amongst whom he administered justice. The litigation related to a certain jade idol, of much sanctity and renown, and one of the main questions involved was the legitimacy of its descent. The evidence adduced in order to verify the sacred image was not, to Norris's mind, satisfactory. In his opinion it ought to have been made an exhibit to an affidavit, and this formality had for some superstitious reason been omitted. The judge very properly insisted upon the idol being brought into court, and then and there had his own initials stamped upon the most protuberant part of its sacred form. Unfortunately this decoration did not commend itself to the taste of the priestly litigants; and the Governor-General and the

Secretary of State for India were put to considerable trouble in consequence. It is difficult to say how much those initials ultimately cost the British tax-payer; and it would be unfair to assume that the frontier operations which took place in the following year were wholly due to this cause. The rules of British jurisprudence were, however, effectively vindicated.

Amongst the most junior of all at the date referred to, the name of C. W. Mathews (now Sir Charles Mathews, Director of Public Prosecutions) cannot be passed over in silence. He had only been a member of the circuit for a year or two, but had already compelled attention, and his fervid eloquence soon became the admiration and despair of his rivals and contemporaries. He was the only advocate I have ever known who could really make a juryman shed tears; and on one occasion, at least, I have seen him perform the same operation in cold blood upon a reluctant judge. Some day, no doubt, his own reminiscences will be published; and if the advance sheets were only available to the present writer, this little volume would need no padding. I may perhaps be permitted, without entirely forfeiting his friendship, to relate a simple anecdote of his prowess. It was at Winchester assizes; and Mathews was addressing a common jury in a torrent of burning eloquence, probably incomprehensible to most of them, but not the less impressive, while he pointed the finger of scorn at the unhappy prosecuting counsel, who sat cowering at his side. "Go it, little un," roared an excited and sympathetic farmer from the body of the court, in the midst of his longest and most incoherent sentence. "Turn that man out of court!" said Mr. Justice Stephen sternly; and operations were suspended for some minutes while this direction was being carried into effect. When order was at length restored, and the audience had settled down into terrified attention, the judge addressed the advocate in dignified and encouraging tones. "Go on, Mr. Mathews, if you please—*exactly where you left off!*"

The advocates whom I have named were in due course succeeded by others, though leaders at the Bar can hardly be considered an ephemeral race, as the generations of men go. I recollect hearing Cole at a circuit dinner, responding as chairman to the toast of his health. He was then in the sere and yellow

D

leaf, and said with some pathos that he knew there were many younger men who thought that King Cole had reigned long enough. No doubt he had served a weary apprenticeship, as he could have had but little encouragement while Cockburn, Coleridge, Karslake, and Montague Smith were in the field. Lopes had already gone to the Bench ; and the leadership was soon divided between Collins and Arthur Charles. Pinder, as has been already mentioned, died suddenly after having sent in his application for silk ; but scarcely any one had seemed to his contemporaries more likely to reach the judicial Bench. Bucknill, Phillimore, Pitt-Lewis, Bompas, Poole, Norris, Petheram, and Warry are the names next in order upon the circuit roll. The two first are now judges of the High Court, and may fairly be regarded as youthful still. In those days they were positively juvenile—at times infantine ; and it seemed but a short time since they were schoolboys at Westminster together. Bompas, who afterwards obtained a County Court judgeship, was the kindest-hearted of men, but affected rather the heavy father during his leadership of the mess. He was the son of the original

from whom Dickens modelled Serjeant
Buzfuz—who was, as every one knows, a prominent member of the Western Circuit.
There appeared not long ago in a daily paper
a statement that His Honour Judge Bompas
had recently presented a lock of the Serjeant's
hair to the Dickens Fellowship. The original
warming-pan, which Mrs. Bardell was implored
not to forget, has long stood on the landing of
a West-Country hotel frequented by the Bar
mess. It should be purchased, in order to
make the gift complete.

Collins, Norris, and Petheram, as has been
mentioned on a previous page, went eventually to the Indian Bench. A. R. Poole, originally a Bristol local, and afterwards Recorder of that city, died at a comparatively early
age, to the great regret of his many friends.
He had rowed twice in the Oxford boat at
Putney, when the Dark Blue successes were
at their zenith; and as a junior enjoyed a
tremendous practice at Bristol and in the
neighbouring counties. As a silk he had
barely time to establish himself, but for some
unexplained reason made a rather slow beginning (for so good an oarsman), which he took
unnecessarily to heart. It is, in fact, very

difficult to account for the caprices of fashion, which make or mar so many advocates at the Bar. I remember dining almost alone with a newly fledged silk on the last night of one Bodmin assize, where we had been detained after most of the Bar had departed for Exeter. After dinner we drifted into talking shop, and began speaking of our respective prospects. "Now you're a sensible fellow," said my companion. (It was after more than one glass of circuit port.) " I dare say you could tell me of some little thing in my style of doing work that I might correct. What do you consider my chief fault?" Of course I assured him that he hadn't any; but he was persistent, and returned to the charge again and again, till I weakly yielded. I told him timidly that the only blemish I could discover in his methods was one that was common to most great advocates—he was sometimes just a little too long. "Too long?" he exclaimed with genuine incredulity. "You mean too short!" But I didn't; and after a while I persuaded him that I was in earnest. He fell to biting his whiskers, which was an oratorical trick he had cultivated, and I could see that he was getting a little morose. So I appealed to his better nature, and reminded him that he had invited the candour of a friend. I added, plaintively, that I should never be offended if he told me of *my* faults. At this he brightened up considerably, and I could see that I was on the road to atone for my indiscretion. " My dear boy," he said with kindly emphasis, " I don't really think that you have a fault. *Except, you know, that you are so d——d offensive !*" I trust that this just criticism has not betrayed the carefully guarded anonymity of the present work.

No man ever left the circuit with a higher reputation than Arthur Charles ; and the ill-health which terminated so prematurely his judicial career was a public calamity, as well as a grief to his many old friends and admirers. It is the wholesome custom on the circuit of which I write to entertain the judges of assize on Grand Night, whenever either judge is an old member of the mess ; and I well remember the occasion—I think there was but one—when Mr. Justice Charles was our welcome guest. One of his successors, whom I have named above, was in the chair ; and it fell to his lot to propose the

D 2

toast of the judge's health. He said much that was true of the services which our visitor had rendered to the circuit, and of the admirable way in which he had formerly discharged his duties as president of the mess. " I have been so long accustomed," he said, " to see our old friend Charles occupying this chair, that I feel some diffidence in assuming this position in his presence. I cannot help feeling that he ought to be in my place—and I in his! " The shouts of laughter which greeted this naive confession rendered inaudible the hurried explanation which no doubt followed. It is not given to every one to veil his aspirations with so much modesty.

.   .   .   .   .   .

The most important social functionary of the circuit has always been, and still is, the Wine Treasurer. He is practically the guardian, and theoretically the sole depositary, of that unwritten code of honourable etiquette to which the circuit attaches so much importance. In the financial and administrative duties of his position—by no means inconsiderable—he is assisted by a small committee ; but so far as his more important functions are concerned, he is theoretically despotic. In order to become a member of the mess, it was (and still is) necessary to obtain an introduction to this high dignitary, and to be proposed under his auspices for election at the next Grand Night—held alternatively at Exeter and Bristol. Should the neophyte desire to attend at any of the earlier towns on the same circuit, he is permitted to do so, and even to dine at mess, in anticipation of this formality. The holder of the office when I first remember the circuit was one Jimmy Hooper (afterwards a County Court judge). It was from him I learned that I should have to make a speech on the night of my election, and that the proper pronunciation of the word " circuit " was " sarkit." I do not know from what century this traditional pronunciation had been handed down; but I regret to say that Jimmy Hooper was the last of a long line of Wine Treasurers who never called it anything else. Since the Judicature Acts came into operation, the time-hallowed pronunciation has been discontinued. Like the conventional " If your ludship pleases," it has become archaic. Jimmy Hooper has had a good many successors, but with the exception of Sir Charles Mathews, who was Wine Treasurer for a brief period in the eighties, none of them achieved much forensic fame. The duties of the post are in fact too onerous to be undertaken by a man of any considerable practice; and when business comes to the holder, the circuit has to find a successor. Most of the other circuits have a similar official, though in some the actual junior for the time being acts as agent and secretary to the anonymous seniors behind him.

The Western Circuit had, however, one institution peculiar to itself. I refer to the Circuit Van, which was an enormous vehicle like those used for the removal of furniture, and was always conveyed at very considerable expense, by rail or road, wherever the assizes were being held. Its primary and nominal use was to convey the "book-boxes" of those barristers who desired to take part of their library with them; and forty years ago there were many such. The beneficent operation of the Judicature Acts has altered all this; and no young barrister of any self-respect requires any other volumes on circuit than Archbold's *Criminal Practice* and the White

Book. These can be, and generally are, borrowed in court from the kindly Clerk of Assize. The further consideration of a case in town, if not unknown then, was at any rate very unusual; and no man with any business thought it safe to travel without at least a hundredweight of legal literature of his own to fall back upon. I know one man who cherishes his "book-box" still, but it rests in well-earned retirement in his country house; and few of the present generation can ever have seen one. One man I remember who had his "book-box" constructed in the shape of a coffin; but he was a sufferer from bibliomania in an advanced stage.

The Circuit Van became gradually degraded into a mere receptacle of ordinary luggage, and there must be many occupants of chambers in the Temple even now who can recollect seeing it standing in Brick Court for some days before the commencement of each assize. Eventually it was decided that the expense of maintaining this ancient institution was inconsistent with the modern demand for champagne every night at mess, and the van itself was sold to a travelling menagerie. The title of "baggage-master," once appurtenant to the care of the van, was retained for a short period by one of the Wine Committee; and one former holder of that rank still adorns the circuit, though shorn of his name and dignity. But when the writer first joined the profession, the abolition of the Circuit Van seemed at least as improbable as the laying of sacrilegious hands upon the Long Vacation.

The records of the circuit show that its numerical strength (now about two hundred and fifty) has steadily increased. In 1824, when one Thomas Erskine was Wine Treasurer, the number on the roll was but seventy-three, amongst the names being those of Wilde, Coleridge, Cresswell, Crowder, and Gaselee. The last-named was raised to the Bench that same year, where he served Charles Dickens as the model for Stareleigh, J., and tried the *cause célèbre* of *Bardell v. Pickwick*. Even in 1852 the number was only eighty-two, and does not seem to have varied much in the years between. That so large a proportion out of this list should have attained distinction is no doubt mainly attributable to the fact that the predecessor of Thomas Erskine in 1823 laid down three whole pipes of 1820 port. He was not only a judge of wine, but a statistician;

and we learn from him that the average consumption of wine on each circuit for the three years ending with 1822 was thirty-seven dozen. It would be invidious to draw any comparison in this respect between the present and the past; but as the largest share was drunk at the Somersetshire and Devonshire assizes, it is permissible to infer that Grand Night was held alternately in those two counties, as it still is. Port, sherry, and Madeira were the wines most favoured; claret seems never to have been a circuit favourite; and the first introduction of champagne at the mess-table took place within the recollection of the present generation. It may be only a coincidence that the decadence of modern oratory, in the riper judgment of those veterans who still survive, dates from about the same time.

.   .   .   .   .   .

Of those who still tread the ancient road— *et quasi cursores vitai lampada tradunt*—I have abstained from speaking. Let not all of them, however, assume that a dread of the law of libel has been the only restraining cause. There are many to whom their own self-respect will suggest, I am sure, a better explanation.

It will, at any rate, be generally admitted that there is no other profession in which men are so ready and generous in their appreciation of their fellows ; nor is this solely due to that species of vanity which seeks consolation for defeat by magnifying the prowess of the victor. On the contrary, it has often happened that a man has acquired the reputation of being a good lawyer by merely demonstrating that he was a bad speaker. There can, however, be no indiscretion in saying that the difference between the circuit mess as I first knew it and the same institution as it exists at present is very marked. In those days a considerable number of barristers of all ages regularly went to circuit, not only without any business to do, but without the slightest desire of obtaining any. Forty or fifty men would in those days sit down at dinner on the first business night at a small assize town, where a quarter of that number is now regarded as more than an average attendance. As a natural consequence, the social side of circuit life was much more developed then than it is at present. The circuit mess had a well-established and permanent cricket club ; and three matches at least (at Winchester, Dorchester, and Exeter) were usually played. At the first one I witnessed the clerk of assize made quite a respectable score. He was the son of Bovill, Chief Justice of the Common Pleas, and had been in the Lancers. It was of him that *Punch* wrote that the Chief Justice, desiring to let his son witness a real action, had taken him out of the army and sent him to the Bar. At that date the next assize town in order of time after Dorchester was Exeter; and at the summer assize it was the custom to charter a small steamer at Weymouth, which took a considerable number of briefless ones round by sea to Exmouth or Torquay. It is true that in those days there were more causes and more prisoners for trial; but I do not think that the falling off of business is sufficient to account for the change. The numerical strength of the circuit, on paper, is greater now than ever it was; but I think that the average aspirant who fails to get into work severs his connection with his nominal profession sooner than was the custom thirty or forty years ago. The dusty road of the law is doubtless an easy one from which to stray, with many pleasant lanes and by-paths, to which it owes much of its attractiveness; while the tolls which the circuit wayfarer has to pay have not of late been lessened. A learned judge was once asked by an anxious mother whether he considered the Bar a good profession for her boy to adopt. "Nothing could be better," responded the veteran. "He can always be certain of a couple of hundred a year at that." "In what manner do you mean?" asked the lady anxiously. "By leaving it off, madam!" was the grim reply. In this way I have seen much money made upon the Western Circuit.

CHAPTER III

SESSIONS

THE first business of the newly fledged barrister, after becoming a member of the circuit, is to attach himself to a particular county sessions. As all the quarter sessions in counties are held in the same week, determined by statute, he is restricted by necessity, as well as custom, to a single county; but he may "open" as many borough sessions as he chooses, these being held on all sorts of varying dates, usually fixed by the Recorder to suit his own convenience. No member of the circuit may take a brief at any county sessions except his own, or at any borough sessions which he has not "opened," without a special fee, the amount of which varies on the different circuits. In each of the principal counties there is a sessions mess, to which it is practically necessary for the newcomer to be elected; but this is not so as a rule with boroughs, though all the barristers attending borough sessions usually belong to the sessions mess of the same county. The sessions mess is quite independent of the circuit mess, and usually makes its own regulations as to special fees and other matters of etiquette without reference to the larger body. Cases even occur now and then where a candidate, after obtaining admission to the circuit mess, has not been elected by the sessions to which he has applied. There is, of course, no law to prevent any man who has been called to the Bar from coming into any court either at assizes or sessions without obtaining the permission of his fellows. In fact, more than one case has occurred within my own memory, where a barrister who had resigned his membership of the mess continued to practise—or rather tried to practise—on the circuit. It is, however, generally understood that those who belong to the regular mess will not hold briefs with an outsider, and in practice membership of the mess has come to be essential. It will thus be readily understood that members of the same sessions mess are thrown into very familiar relations with each other. With these explanatory remarks, which are intended for the benefit of unprofessional readers only, it may, I hope, prove interesting to give some account of the prominent members of the Devon sessions, when the author joined that celebrated body at a date which may be roughly indicated as Early Victorian.

Senior of all, even then, was a notable prisoners' advocate, who spoke in the broadest Devonshire, and had been known to West-Country folk for many years as Counsellor Carter. It was popularly said that in his early days he had defended two of the Doones of Exmoor. I believed it then ; and though we have since been taught that there never were any Doones, and I have seen for myself that there is no Doone Valley, I may be allowed to believe it still. Samuel Carter had been elected member for Tavistock in 1852 as an advanced Radical, and he made one speech in the House of Commons which, at any rate, achieved notoriety. It was in opposition to the vote for the public funeral of the Duke of Wellington, which Carter objected to as a scandalous waste of public money, and the curious may find it in the pages of Hansard for November 16th, 1852 (Vol. CXXIII, p. 213).

E

Those who care to look for and read it will readily understand the storm of indignation which one expression at once aroused. It was soon discovered that the speaker was not possessed of the property qualification then required for membership of the House of Commons, and he paid the penalty of his indiscretion by losing his seat. He had, in truth, the bitterest of tongues, and always seemed to glory in the unconventional violence of his language. Even the judges fought shy of an encounter with so doughty and implacable an opponent. "Mr. Carter, you are wasting the time of the court!" said Blackburn, J., once to him at Bodmin. "Time of the court!" retorted the truculent veteran, glaring fiercely at the Bench. "Your Lordship means—your Lordship's dinner!" The judge threw up his hands in despair—one could almost hear him appealing to Heaven—and Carter continued his harangue. It is really difficult to see what more the judge could have done. To have committed the offender, or to have adjourned the court, would have been only a temporary expedient, and something worse would inevitably have followed on the next day. Besides, it was undeniably true that it was nearly seven o'clock. At any rate, Carter proceeded with his speech in triumph, and finally crowned his iniquities by obtaining for his client a most unrighteous acquittal. The same redoubtable advocate was on another occasion defending a man at the assizes on a charge of obtaining money by false pretences. "False pretences!" said Carter, with fine scorn. "Why, we all make them every day! barristers and solicitors and judges—the whole lot of us. Talk of the purity of the judicial ermine!" Here he pointed derisively at the learned judge who sat cowering on the Bench. "Why, it's only rabbit-skin!" Shouts of laughter greeted this irreverent statement, which indeed I suspect to be literally true.

The most outrageous utterance, however, that I ever heard from the lips of this picturesque old savage was at Exeter. It was in the Criminal Court, one summer assizes, and Carter was cross-examining a farmer's wife who had sworn to the identity of some stolen ducks. The afternoon was hot, and the good lady, a little flustered by her position, was adjusting a bonnet which sat somewhat uneasily at the back of her head. She was recalled to an attitude of strict attention by the following polished rebuke : " When you've *caught* it, ma'am," said Carter in a tone of brutal irony, " I'll go on ! "

It may be imagined by those who remember Lord Coleridge (the late Lord Chief Justice), that when he was a junior with Samuel Carter on the Devon sessions they were not exactly congenial spirits. Upon one occasion, long before the time of which I write, when they were opposed to each other in a criminal case, Carter remarked pleasantly to the jury, as a relevant fact bearing upon the question of the prisoner's innocence, that though Mr. Coleridge was not himself a Jesuit, his brother was ! This was Carter's amiable way of emphasizing the fact that one of the Coleridge family had entered the Roman Catholic Church ; but one can understand that the incident was not exactly conducive to good feeling. Still, it is scarcely an adequate explanation of the welcome which was offered by Counsellor Carter to Bernard Coleridge (as he then was) when he made his first appearance on the Devon sessions at a much later date. Bernard Coleridge had been entrusted with his first prosecution, and Carter was defending in his usual energetic and rambling style. There was little to be said in favour of the prisoner, and his counsel was driven—as better men before him have been—to discuss somewhat immaterial topics. Having addressed the court for some time on the subjects of Church disestablishment, the price of bread, and the game laws, he next turned the stream of his eloquence on his youthful opponent. " Mr. Coleridge is prosecuting this unhappy man!" said Carter to the jury with indignation. " I remember his grandfather on these same sessions!" (This referred to Sir John Coleridge, who was appointed a judge of the Queen's Bench in 1835, but Carter found no difficulty in looking back fifty years or so.) " Well—he's dead—and I won't say anything more about *him*. Then came his son, whom we all remember well enough—and they made him Lord Chief Justice! Now here's another of 'em!" One of the few survivors who witnessed this scene gives me as a variant, " And they ain't done coming yet!" But I think my own memory is the more accurate of the two. I did not know then, any more than did the speaker, that I should live to see the third of the Coleridges, after presiding in that very court as chairman of quarter sessions, taking his seat there as one of His Majesty's judges of assize. But when that time came, the satisfaction of the Bar was tinged with something of regret. It was almost a tragedy that Samuel Carter should not have survived, in order to defend one more unhappy man before his hereditary antagonist. Enough, perhaps, has now been written of Counsellor Carter.

Next among the veterans of the Devon sessions in the seventies came one Henry Clark. Clark lived upon a small estate of his own in the neighbourhood of Plymouth, and was by nature and habit not a lawyer at all, but a country squire and sportsman. He was the best fisherman and one of the best shots in Devonshire; and must have been personally acquainted with almost every magistrates' clerk in the county. The result of these qualifications was that he had more prosecutions to conduct at sessions and assizes than any other member of the Bar, and the assistance of a "devil" was frequently an absolute necessity to him. In this humble capacity I was fortunate enough to be of some use, and he was desirous of making me some acknow-

ledgment of my services. He told me that
he was possessed of an invaluable formula for
the examination-in-chief of a police constable,
and volunteered to communicate to me what
he described as the secret of his professional
success. "Three questions, my dear boy, or
at the most four, will take you safely
through any case you're likely to get. Copy
them into the fly-leaf of your 'Archbold,'
and you'll never find yourself in a difficulty."
I opened my copy of that indispensable text-
book and dipped my pen in the ink. The
first question, he said, need not be answered.
It was, "You are a police constable of the
county of Devon, stationed at X?" The
second question was, "What do you know
about this case?" The witness, said my
mentor, will then begin to repeat his proof.
"If he sticks at any part of it, you should say,
'Go on'; when he comes to a full stop, you
wind up with the final question, 'You've forgotten something, haven't you?' If the
prisoner isn't convicted after that, it won't be
your fault." Equipped with this armoury, it
is indeed obvious that the young barrister may
go far. Henry Clark, however, had many
better qualities than those of an advocate, and

my gratitude to him for other real kindnesses should be here recorded.

The " Saint " was another well-known member of the sessions who has passed away. He bore a name which was itself a passport to popularity in the West of England ; and was the inventor of an original defence in certain cases of assault, which he exploited with considerable success. On circuit he is probably best remembered by his admirable rendering of " The Poacher " on Grand Night, which he performed up to the last year of his life as tunefully as ever. His most celebrated song, however, was entitled " Penal Servitude," which he gave as if to the manner born. Neither the words nor the music, to the best of my belief, are to be found in print ; but if they are, I may possibly confer a public benefit by unearthing the owner of the copyright. In this hope I append the first three or four stanzas, which are all that I have been able to rescue from oblivion. Perhaps some musical and poetical genius will revive the ditty, before circuits pass away and Grand Nights become as obsolete as Arabian ones. No one, I trust, will detect where a failing memory has been supplemented by poetic invention.

PENAL SERVITUDE

1. O, I've just come back from Australia!
     Where I've been for a little change of air;
   An', ole pals, on the quiet I can tell yer,
     There's lots of decent living over there.
   For they feeds yer—an' they clothes yer—
   Yer lives better than a working man or sojer.
   Oho! oho! oho! penal servitude's the sort of life
       for me!
   For yer does a little work jes' a portion of the day,
               (*Treadmill action with hands here.*)
   An' then yer goes to church upon a Sunday.
   Oho! oho! oho-ho!
   Penal servitude's the sort of life for me!

2. I was tried one day at the Old Bailey,
     The jury found me guilty, I believe!
   An' across the sea for seven years they sent me!
     But I soon got a ticket, boys, of leave.
           For they, etc.

3. It doesn't matter now what I was sent for,
     I was always up to every sort of game;
   I've got a tidy number to repent for,
     So you needn't trouble much about the name!
           For they, etc.

4. The beaks and the parsons go on preachin',
     If they were dumb it wouldn't be no loss;
   There isn't any use in all their teachin',
     For the blokes that gets their livin' on the cross.
           For they, etc.

5. So d——n the judge, I says, and blast the jury,
    They're a lot of bally cowards every one ;
An' if they'd 'arf the pluck, I do assure ye,
    They'd do the very same as I have done.
        For they, etc.

It is essential, in order to convey the effect of the above Bowdlerized lines (which I have heard sung before a Lord Chief Justice of England), that some idea of the air should be given ; and the indulgence of all musicians is craved for the subjoined effort at its reproduction.

In the days when these worthies flourished, the decadence of business at quarter sessions had already commenced, and it was by no means easy for a new-comer to gain a footing. There were very few prisoners, and of course still fewer appeals ; and a junior thought himself lucky if, in return for his expenditure in railway fares and hotel expenses, he was rewarded with a guinea brief to apply for a knacker's licence. I remember, however, one memorable stroke of luck which befell a beginner whom we will call Tompkins, the history of which may be worth recording. One of the great railway companies brought some appeals against the rating of parts of

"Penal Servitude."

Vivace.

O! I'm just come back from Aus-tra-lia! Where I've been for a lit-tle change of

air! An', ole pals, on the qui-et I can tell yer, There's

lots of decent liv-ing o-ver there! For they feeds yer, An' they clothes yer! Ye lives

better than a working-man or sol-dier !   O - ho,   o - ho,   o - ho !   Pe - nal

ser - vi - tude's the sort of life for me !   For ye does a lit - tle work just a
(Treadmill action with the hands here.)

portion of the day, An' then ye goes to church upon a Sun - day !   O - ho,

o - ho,   o - ho - ho !   Pe - nal servitude's the sort of life for me !

their line, which it was intended ultimately to refer. In the meantime a junior had to be briefed to enter and respite them at sessions ; and for reasons which will presently appear, Tompkins was selected for this task. There were eight appeals originally, for eight separate parishes ; but the number doubled itself automatically every time a fresh rate was made ; and in this way the total rose in successive half-years to sixteen, thirty-two, and finally sixty-four. As each respite of each appeal involved a guinea brief, in addition to vast possibilities if any of them was ever tried, it will be seen that Tompkins had got hold of a very good thing. That these briefs were obtained quite legitimately I need hardly say ; but beginners at the Bar may like to know how it was done. They will find that the procedure of Tompkins may be readily and profitably followed by any intelligent man.

There was at that time on the circuit a man who shall be called Jones, though in fact he bore a more distinguished name. He had been frequently briefed by the railway company in question in the county courts, and even in assize cases ; and he set great store by the possession of so valuable a client. He was also a bit of

a pessimist, like many other excellent people ;
and Tompkins was present one evening, when
he was indulging this idiosyncrasy in a sitting-
room shared by half a dozen other juniors at
Bristol. "You have no reason to grumble,
at any rate," said Tompkins reprovingly.
"You must have made at least three hundred last year out of your railway company
alone." Tompkins had in fact no knowledge
on the subject, and was speaking on mere
conjecture ; but it became evident from Jones's
halting disclaimer that the shot was a good
one. "Of course I am speaking in round
numbers," said Tompkins in a tone of quiet
confidence. "I am aware that your fees fell
short of that sum by ten or twelve pounds."
"Who told you that ?" asked Jones, looking
a little startled. "Oh, it was old C.," said
Tompkins carelessly, naming at random the
solicitor to the railway company. "*You*
don't know old C.," said Jones, with some
perturbation, feeling that his own relations
with that excellent client were in jeopardy.
"Not know old C. !" exclaimed Tompkins,
who had all the virtues except veracity.
"Why, when I was at school at Grey Friars,
I used to spend my *exeat* Sundays down at

his place. I am not sure that he isn't my godfather!" Jones looked still more annoyed, but said nothing more. Next time, however, that he met the eminent solicitor in question, he asked him if he knew much of Tompkins. "Never heard of him in my life," answered that important personage. "You must have forgotten him," said Jones sadly. "He used to come to your house when he was a school-boy, and he thinks you're his godfather." "You don't say so!" said C., who had a good heart. "I'd quite forgotten it. I suppose I must send him a brief," and he did. So it was really to Jones that the unveracious Tompkins was indebted for his geometrical progression of rating appeals.

This was a bow drawn at a venture. A learned judge, to whom I afterwards told the story, said that it reminded him of the death of Ahab, as narrated by an undergraduate in his answers to an examination paper in Scripture history. "Ahab was one day driving in his chariot, when he met a man who was out venture-shooting. The man shot at a venture, and missed it, but he hit Ahab." He added in a footnote, for the benefit of the ignorant examiner, that a "venture" was a kind of small

antelope, found only in the hills of Palestine.
So did Tompkins inadvertently bring down
the railway solicitor, when drawing the long-
bow for the benefit of Jones. A day's venture-
shooting is not always waste of time, if you
have the good fortune to find yourself on the
hills of Palestine.

. . . . . .

Sessions, though still a good "jumping-off
ground," have lost much of their former importance. The main cause of this is, of course,
the increased jurisdiction of the magistrates,
who now deal summarily with a large number
of cases which were formerly sent for trial.
Even large counties now often have less than
a dozen prisoners at quarter sessions, with
a Bar numbering between twenty and thirty
waiting anxiously to divide the spoil. Trial
of an indictable offence before a jury is considerably more costly than the simpler procedure before justices ; and in some places, at
any rate, I think there is a feeling in the minds
of the magistrates' clerks that this expense
ought to be cut down as far as possible. The
civil work at sessions has also shown a strong
tendency to diminish, and the happening of

such a windfall of rating appeals as has been just recorded is, of course, the event of a life-time. In former years appeals in pauper settlement cases formed a large proportion of the business in the civil court. I was told by an old solicitor, that he remembered when he was a clerk delivering no less than seventy briefs of this class at one sessions to Cockburn — afterwards, of course, the Lord Chief Justice — and he said that this was not regarded at the time as anything out of the way. Altera-tions in the statute-book have almost put an end to this kind of litigation—very much to the advantage of the public—and many ex-perienced sessions lawyers of the present day hardly know what a settlement appeal is. Licensing appeals were for some time fairly plentiful after the general licensing meeting in each year; but the effect of the last Licensing Act has been to withdraw most of them from the Quarter Sessions Court. On the whole, the junior barristers who attend county sessions have a poor time of it as compared with their predecessors of half a century ago. It is still, however, an invaluable training-ground for the young practitioner; and I have always thought that those who attained judicial office of any

F

kind without having enjoyed the experience of sessions were placed at a considerable disadvantage. Even magistrates are none the worse for a little practical acquaintance with the rules of evidence and procedure, and it is a common thing for young men who have the prospect of settling down as county gentlemen to attend sessions for a few years, with the idea of qualifying themselves for that position. It is quite certain that if a magistrate does not acquire a little law before he takes his seat on the bench, he will not learn much afterwards, and magistrates' clerks are not always infallible. If the Lord Chancellor could only institute some sort of qualifying examination before new magistrates were appointed, I am sure that the difficulties he has to contend with in discharging this burdensome duty at present would be much diminished. It cannot be denied, however, that this would be the thin edge of a dangerous wedge. Some rash iconoclast might arise to demand the application of a similar test to the County Court Bench. This would be irreverence indeed—a step further would be profane.

.   .   .   .   .   .

There were certainly four, and to the best of my recollection, six standing chairmen of the Devon quarter sessions thirty or forty years ago. The venerable and universally esteemed Earl of Devon usually presided in one court, where he gave invariable satisfaction, though somewhat handicapped by his strong facial resemblance to Counsellor Carter, whose peculiarities have been already chronicled. In the second court the chair was generally taken by a prebendary, somewhat advanced in years, of blameless life and prebendarial reputation. I well remember his being addressed by a junior barrister, for whom as much could not be said, in an appeal against a bastardy order. "You and I, sir, as men of the world, know how difficult it is to refute a charge of this description!" The reverend chairman clutched the arms of his chair convulsively, but restrained himself like a man, and eventually dismissed the appeal with dignity, though not on the grounds suggested by the learned counsel. Both the prebendary and Lord Devon were men of great experience—of greater value to a chairman of quarter sessions than much legal learning. I was once present when a country gentleman, whose only qualification was that he had once been called to the Bar, sat in the capacity of chairman for the first time. He tried six cases that day, all undefended, and every one of them resulted in an acquittal. One of them—a charge of stealing potatoes—will be sufficient as an illustration. Several hundredweight of potatoes had been taken, and the prisoner had been seen in the early hours of the morning, loading them from the prosecutor's loft into his own cart. He was taken "red-handed" by a policeman, who had been watching from behind a hedge, and the farmer who had grown the potatoes was called to prove that they were his property. When the prisoner was invited to cross-examine, he asked the constable if he had not said, when being arrested, that the potatoes were of the same variety as his own. The witness answered curtly that he had said nothing at all, and the prisoner made no further attempt to defend himself. The learned chairman then proceeded to sum up as follows : " Gentlemen of the jury, this case involves what we lawyers call a conflict of evidence. On the one side you have the evidence of the prosecutor and the policeman, to which you will give such weight as you think it deserves.

On the other side you have the prisoner saying, or rather suggesting by his cross-examination that he would say, if his mouth was not
closed, that he thought the potatoes were his
own. It is, of course, for the prosecution to
make out their case, and it is my duty to tell
you that the prisoner is entitled to the benefit
of any reasonable doubt. Gentlemen, consider
your verdict." The new chairman had been
carefully coached, and his instructor had
warned him to introduce the above two pro-
positions of law into every summing-up.
Coming on top of the " conflict of evidence,"
they were too much for the jury, and the
prisoner was acquitted. A little less learning
and a little more experience would have taught
the chairman that these undeniably sound
maxims should be handled with a more deli-
cate touch.

The art of summing-up discreetly to a jury is
in truth a somewhat rare endowment at quarter
sessions. Even amongst His Majesty's judges
there are degrees of excellence. It has always
appeared to me that a well-known example,
usually attributed to Mr. Justice Maule, might
be adapted with great advantage for ordinary
use. " Gentlemen of the jury," he is reported

to have once said, "if you believe the witnesses for the plaintiff, you will find for the defendant. If you believe the witnesses for the defendant, you will find for the plaintiff. If, like myself, you don't believe any of them, Heaven knows which way you will find. Consider your verdict."

A still more concise summing-up in a civil case has been attributed to Baron Bramwell. The defendant's counsel closed his case without calling a witness whose coming had been much expected. "Don't you call Jones, Mr. Blank?" said the judge significantly at the close of counsel's address. "I do not, my lord," replied the advocate. The judge turned round to the jury and gave vent to a low and prolonged whistle. "Whe-e-ew," he said, or rather whistled. "Gentlemen, consider your verdict." This is probably the shortest and most intelligible example on record. It has, at any rate, the merit—not the most conspicuous feature of the modern practice—of distinguishing accurately between law and fact.

It is perhaps natural that recorders should be more wisely chary than sessions chairmen of displaying their store of legal learning in court. I remember an occasion in my early days when I appeared at a borough sessions in an appeal against an order of justices on purely legal grounds. When the court adjourned for lunch the appeal had just started, and the learned Recorder invited all the counsel in the case to see him in his private room. " Look here, you fellows," he said, as soon as we were in that safe retreat. "This case seems to me to depend upon a point of law. Now don't let us make d——d fools of ourselves over it in court—why can't we settle it in here ? " It was impossible for us to resist this appeal, and judicial modesty had to be humoured accordingly. We were all afraid then of others seeing us as we saw ourselves. As we learn to appreciate our own intelligence better, we become conscious that this is almost too much to hope for.

If recorders mistrust their own law, they may, at any rate, cherish the hope that their legal attainments are sometimes underrated by the public, if not by the Bar. One of the first defences I remember to have had was at a small borough sessions, where a deputy-recorder was sitting for the occasion. The clerk of the peace had drawn an indictment for larceny, and had added a count for false pretences—in order to be, as he fondly imagined, on the safe side. The solicitor for the defence knew more than he did, and called my attention to the irregularity of joining a misdemeanour and a felony in the same indictment. The objection was taken and proved fatal; and as the grand jury had been discharged, no other bill could be sent up to them. "That comes of having a deputy-recorder," observed the mortified clerk of the peace, by no means inaudibly. "Our own Recorder—he never pays no attention to such nonsense." The lawyer for whom the technicalities of antiquity have a fascination may still occasionally find gratification for his tastes in the criminal court; but even there the hand of the iconoclast will make itself felt. I remember a technical objection being taken at assizes to the form of an indictment against a corporation for non-repair of a highway. The presiding judge listened with scornful impatience to the argument, and then curtly announced that any amendment necessary to secure a conviction must be taken as made. Though the High Sheriff sat in uniform by his side, he still fondly fancied he was in the Commercial Court—the garden which he loved!

"CIRCUIT GHOSTS"

Long the day has been and weary, and the pathway
    somewhat rough ;

Steep the hills, and hot the noontide ; many slips, and
    falls enough !

Yet at times my restless fancy seeks the journey to
    retrace,

Fills the silent years with voices, peoples every empty
    place,

Smiles at jests whose mirth has perished, mourns at
    sorrows long consoled,

Goes again the Western Circuit, as we went in days
    of old.

Once again I sit and listen, empty hands and pockets
    bare,

Smothering a little envy at the briefs that others
    share ;

Once again I smile discreetly on the small attorney's
    clerk,

Once again I gaze complacent at the fee he deigns to
    mark ;

Once again I gasp and falter, stammering with youth
    and shame,

While the clerk of the indictments hands his lordship
    up my name ;

Again I bid the glib policeman faithfully his proof
    repeat,

Again my veteran opponent tramples me beneath his
    feet ;

To my eloquent harangue the jury listen very little,

And my first forensic effort ends again—in an acquittal !

Graver are the dreams that follow, as the brows are
  knit with care,
Lined perhaps a little deeper, and with somewhat less
  of hair ;
Vexed by over-righteous judges, at unrighteous verdicts
  glad,
Overcheered by scanty triumphs, at reverses oversad.
Onward with remorseful glances, as the years go wasted
  by,
Still we press, not seeing whither ; still we strive, scarce
  knowing why.
All the day is full of murmurs, all the night alive with
  forms—
Shadows of reproachful clients, echoes of judicial
  storms ;
Cloistered close and running waters, banquetings and
  merry meals,
To the sound of sheriff's trumpets and the clank of
  iron wheels ;
Bloodstained hands and satyr faces, lips that whisper,
  eyes that weep—
Phantoms all, like fading visions half remembered
  after sleep !

Surely others dreamed as we dream, other feet have
  worn the stone,
Other forms have been before us in the seats we call
  our own ;
Other briefs lie on the tables, keeping still their ghostly
  shape,
Briefs endorsed by spirit fingers, neatly tied with
  phantom tape ;
Other causes, other quarrels, other hopes and other
  fears,

Fill the sullen courts with laughter, move the stony
walls to tears.
Names are we, and voices only, passing on our little
round,
Words that perish all our labour, all our toil an
empty sound.
In the dark and hurrying Future, the inheritors of Life,
Outstretched hands, uplifted faces, wait their summons
to the strife :
They shall wake the solemn echoes, they shall tread
the ancient street,
Hastening from court to lodging—fresher voices,
younger feet ;
Then our boyhood's labours ended, ended then our
manhood's boasts,
Shadows whispering from Somewhere, We shall be the
Circuit Ghosts !

CHAPTER IV

THE CIVIL COURT

THE advocate's recollections of the Civil Court are usually more interesting to himself and his clerk than to other people. Wherever and whenever prisoners are being tried, the space allotted to the public is invariably thronged by an uncomfortable and unsavoury crowd ; to say nothing of the inevitable bevy of lady spectators who are wont to adorn the precincts of the Bench itself, until they are invited for their own sakes to withdraw. Nearly every one, I imagine, feels that he has the potentialities of a criminal within him ; while nobody ever expects to become a plaintiff or a defendant, and very few do—to their own great loss and that of the Bar. I never met but one litigant who could honestly say that he liked it, though some are partially consoled by the greater sufferings of their opponents. The few eccentric persons who take a real delight in the fray too often degenerate into mere litigants in person ; and I am sure that such enjoy themselves greatly, though they give no pleasure to other people. The Civil Court is for these and other reasons a place of gloom ; and though the judges do their best to enliven it, they are usually repressed by the solemnity of the advocates. The " importance of being earnest " is, in my humble judgment, much overrated by modern professors ; and the possession of what may be described as a " good graveside manner " is too often regarded nowadays as the barrister's most valuable asset. I cannot help thinking that if a little trouble were taken to make the trial of actions more attractive to the public, we should hear fewer complaints of the decline of civil business on circuit.

There is, unfortunately, no doubt that such a decline has taken place, though my diagnosis of its causes may not be exhaustive. An analysis of the cause-lists would, I think, show that more actions are brought for slander or libel than for any other cause ; though it is to be regretted that the Bench gives little encouragement to this particular branch of litigation—almost the only one which would

show, under proper cultivation, a healthy
growth. It may be conceded that such
actions are often called trivial, and even
trumpery; but these are but relative terms,
after all; and if the mountain only gives birth
to a mouse, when rats are looked for, the
mouse is entitled to be caught. The amount
of hatred, passion, malice, and uncharitableness
which gives rise to an action for defamation
does not all depend upon the vulgarity or
pettiness of the abuse complained of; and it
is these very manifestations of the Evil One
which the beneficent action of the law, by the
cold douche of justice, is intended to subdue.
I remember once hearing Serjeant Ballantine
say, in answer to an inquiry as to the nature
of the case on which he was engaged, "Oh, it
is the usual thing. My client has been convicted three times of fraud, and now brings
his action, very properly, to vindicate his
character." The nobility of the purpose, and
not the magnitude of the provocative cause,
was to that great lawyer the true measure of
his task. In those days advocates were not
ashamed to speak of the reputation of the
poorest client in terms which would now be
deemed almost extravagant. "Gentlemen of

the jury," Lord Erskine is reported to have once said at Guildhall, "the reputation of a cheesemonger in the city of London is like the bloom upon a peach. Breathe on it!—and it is gone for ever!" I cannot think of any judge before whom an advocate would now dare to speak with so much boldness. And if it be true, as a late Chief Justice once said, that "most men are what most men think them," surely no plaintiff is to be censured because he desires to teach the defendant to think better of him in the future. He cannot have foreseen that the judge will think worse.

There is, however, one kind of action which will never cease to be popular with the public and the Press; and for that reason, I suppose, periodical attempts are made in Parliament to abolish it. I refer, of course, to actions for breach of promise of marriage. In practice, those which are actually tried are usually of a dull and even commonplace character, while those which might prove interesting to the junior Bar are for the most part settled by the leaders. They may always be relied upon, however, to draw a full house, doubtless because all men enjoy seeing the worm wriggle and hearing the victim bleat. Few indeed are the advocates who can cut a respectable figure when appearing for the worm, which must never be allowed to turn, or it will be all the worse for him. I have seen prodigious damages given as the result of an unsuccessful attack upon the lady's character; and the advocate's best chance is to make her appear ridiculous. The greatest adept at this resource that I remember was Serjeant Parry. There was a case tried at Westminster, some thirty or forty years ago, in which the plaintiff had made the acquaintance of the defendant at the top of Regent Street, and had been promised marriage the same day in a private hotel somewhere near the Strand. The introduction had been effected, according to the lady, by the gentleman offering to protect her against a vicious terrier; and Parry, who appeared for the defendant, had a little misunderstood the story. "You say you were alarmed at two dogs fighting, madam?" he asked her. "No, no," answered the fair plaintiff, "it was a single dog." "What you mean, madam," said Parry, "is that there was only one dog; but *whether it was a single dog or a married dog you are not in a position to say!*" Nor was she, after this correction, in a position to say much more;

and the worm on that occasion got off the hook. Serjeant Parry was an oldish man when I remember him, but to my mind he was the most persuasive advocate that ever addressed a jury. He had not the overwhelming force of Russell, nor the incisive persistence in cross-examination of Hawkins, nor the silver tongue of Coleridge; who were all in their own peculiar style unapproachable. But he had *persuasion*, which, after all, is the end to which other qualities are the means; and I doubt if any advocate of his day could have shown a higher average of successes. Success in winning verdicts is, after all, not the true test of the merits of the advocate. Many men are habitually resorted to in hopeless cases, especially in the criminal court; and every barrister knows that a long sequence of briefs for a defendant makes a very poor showing, if results are looked to. There was a notable advocate in the middle of the last century, called Edward James—not to be confused with Edwin James, from whom Dickens is said to have modelled the character of Stryver, Q.C. I was told by Lord Coleridge, C.J., that Edward James was the best loser he ever knew, and that he would come back from

G

Guildhall after half a dozen defeats, with the same number of grateful clients attached to him for life. This sounds excellently well; but I think most of us would rather win, all the same; and it is a poor consolation, after a series of failures for the defendant, to be reminded that it is always three to one on the plaintiff.

There is probably nothing which has done so much to debase the style of modern advocacy as the introduction of non-jury causes. Since the Judicature Acts came into operation a large number of cases have been tried before a judge alone, and the proportion of these shows a tendency to increase. It is not to be wondered at that the advocate, doing much of his work under these novel conditions, has modified his style accordingly. Evolution has produced a new type, and the common-law leader is no longer of a different species from his brother who practises in equity. The main difference left is that the Chancery silk, who attaches himself to a particular court, has only to mould himself to the idiosyncrasies of one judge. The common-law man, on the other hand, must adapt himself to fifteen, and when he has made a lifelong study of these he may be suddenly confronted with a Chancery judge taking non-juries after all. Such a convulsion of nature might well have disconcerted even an Erskine or a Scarlett. The conduct of a case under these circumstances demands an entirely new set of faculties on the part of an advocate. The man who addresses a jury, however great his experience, never realizes how little they understand of the case. In a "non-jury" the position is reversed—there is always the danger that the judge may understand it all. To attempt eloquence under such circumstances is like dancing in fetters. I knew one orator at the Bar who professed that he always refused briefs in non-jury cases, lest they should spoil his style. It may have been the case, for he certainly seldom appeared in any.

Even before twelve good men and true, the orator of the present day sometimes labours under difficulties. It has happened to the Circuit Tramp, after pouring out his passionate soul before a common jury for, perhaps, twenty minutes, to hear one of the most dignified and kindly of His Majesty's judges commence his summing-up as follows : " Gentlemen of the jury, Mr. Circitor has just addressed you in a very long and most ingenious speech. *You see what I mean?* Now listen to me!" The fame of Demosthenes would hardly have endured for so many centuries, if he had been paid many compliments like this in his lifetime ; and it was a beneficent rule of Greek jurisprudence that closed the mouths of the judges before whom he practised.

The dignitaries of the Common Law Bench, when non-juries were first introduced, at times took strange views of their novel task. I remember one case being tried at Winchester, in which the lady manageress of an hotel sued for slander, the imputation being that she fortified herself for the discharge of her duties with too much liquid. The judge was one of the most learned on the Bench, but he had little or no experience of the standard of temperance applicable to a plaintiff in her position, and he gave judgment as follows : "This case ought to have been tried before a common jury, and I can't conceive why it was not. If it had been, I know what the jury would have said. They would have said so and so, and so and so. *They would have been quite wrong.* But here am I sitting in the place of a common jury ; and I think, on the whole, I ought to find what I believe they would have found." So he found it. I don't know what the unsuccessful litigant thought, but no one else took the learned judge seriously, and the Court of Appeal was not invoked. It would be charitable to assume that he knew more about the subject than he was willing to admit. It will be remembered that Lord Justice Bramwell once asserted in court that one-third of every judge was a common juror, if you got beneath the ermine. So, if you scratch a Russian, it is said that you find a Tartar.

The decadence of the orator is thus the natural consequence of the evolution of the modern trial. Judges sitting without juries, official referees, and professional arbitrators, have curbed the fancy and emasculated the eloquence of the ambitious advocate ; and many a mute, inglorious Erskine has doubtless pined in obscurity, or withered speechless at the portals of the Commercial Court. A very learned official referee is reported lately to have said that the language of metaphor fatigued him ; and even common jurymen, taught by their betters, yawn cynically when the poor flowers of present-day eloquence are offered for their delectation. Thus to find the ideal advocate, one would look for a chartered accountant, accustomed to read the lessons in his parish church.

One true illustration of the helplessness of an advocate in such a position seems worth recording. It was a "light and air" case, sent down from Chancery to be tried on circuit, and was taken before a judge alone—certainly not the course which was contemplated by the Chancery judge who parted with it. The plaintiff's case was closed; and the judge intimated that he would like to go and view the buildings in dispute. The defendant's counsel jumped at the idea, and said with an air of extreme confidence that if his lordship would be good enough to do that, he should not think it necessary to take up time by calling any witnesses. Thereupon the court rose. Next morning the judge announced significantly that he had seen the premises. "Then your lordship has no doubt formed your own opinion," said my sanguine leader, "and in that case any speeches from counsel would be superfluous." So he said nothing; and the judge promptly gave judgment for the plaintiff, with an injunction and costs. This is not the style of oratory which was in vogue before the Judicature Acts, nor do I recommend it even now for general adoption; but there are occasions when it is the only course open to the distracted advocate.

It has naturally happened, that as the practical value of oratory has diminished, so the power of appreciating its beauties—even if confessedly meretricious—has almost died out. Giants there were, no doubt, in the days of old; and much havoc they wrought when they went out to war, belabouring each other with resounding thwacks; but we of to-day find it hard to understand the secret of their prowess. We read the effusions of Erskine, of Brougham, or of Scarlett, without admiration, without emotion, without any sentiment but that of cultured indifference. Take, for instance, Brougham's speech in defence of Queen Caroline, or Burke's impeachment of Warren Hastings, or any of Erskine's incessant invocations of the Deity. Can we honestly say that any of these move us to pity, or quicken us with sympathy, or thrill us with indignation ? " Save the country, my lords, from the horrors of this catastrophe! Save the country, that you may continue to adorn it! Save the throne, which is in jeopardy! the aristocracy, which is shaken!" How turgid it all sounds to us now! how verbose! how unconvincing! It is not that the words are archaic, or that the diction is unfamiliar in our ears. Literature has not suffered the same depreciation as oratory. The Immortals in letters of the eighteenth, the seventeenth, the sixteenth century, are immortal still. Turn to the classics, and the same distinction makes itself felt. "*Eloquium et famam Demosthenis aut Ciceronis Incipit optare,*" says Juvenal of the youthful aspirant to forensic fame. Who can read the Philippics, or the *De Corona,* or the denunciations of Catiline now, and say with truth that he would have recognized the authors as supreme masters of eloquence, if he had not been taught to think so? The scholar can still find pleasure in Cicero the philosopher. The *De Senectute* and the *De Finibus* are still alive with human sympathy; but the Orations have become dry bones, and there is no breath in them.

One explanation of this phenomenon may

perhaps be that the realities of life are essentially transitory. The struggles, the achievements, the virtues, the vices of the past lose something of their interest with every century. Fiction only, and poetry, have the secret of immortality and perpetual youth. Is there anything in ancient history which kindles our imagination, except that which is impossible or untrue ? The legends of Troy, of Ulysses, of ancient Rome, of Olympus and Parnassus —what in comparison with these are the Punic wars, the marchings of Cæsar or of Xenophon, the butcheries of Roman emperors, or the civilization of Europe ? Is there any historical work more appallingly dull than Hallam's *History of the Middle Ages ?* If we turn to the records of our own country, we fail equally to sympathize with or understand the mental attitude of our forefathers. King Alfred and Harold are almost as mythical as Jason ; but the joviality of bluff King Hal, the goodness of Queen Bess, the merriment of Charles the Second, even the " bloodiness " of poor Queen Mary—have they any reality left for us to-day ? Only the dreams of poets have outlived their sepulchres, and the stars of Milton and Shakespeare blaze for ever in eternal sky.

.   .   .   .   .   .

It may be that this digression will be regarded as an inadequate explanation of the degeneracy of the modern orator ; but I can think of no other so little likely to injure his self-respect. There will perhaps be found some to prefer a theory which was lately advanced at a Congress of Head Masters ; to wit, that the decadence of eloquence is directly attributable to the abolition of compulsory Greek.

.   .   ,   .   .   .

It is more difficult to understand another change which has taken place of late years in the trial of civil cases. I mean the increase in their duration. That an action should occupy a judge and jury for a whole week is nowadays considered nothing extraordinary. Most seriously contested special jury cases last a couple of days ; and on circuit one constantly sees the first common jury barely finished at the end of a long day's sitting. One ready mode of explaining this is to set it down to the prolixity of counsel ; and no doubt there are some members of the judicial Bench who are of this opinion. It would be almost as reasonable, in my humble judgment, to attribute it to the increased volume of the judge's notes. The fact is, that the material is usually present in increasing and almost unmanageable quantity, and it becomes necessary to deal with it. There has been an enormous increase in modern times in the habit of letter-writing, both in social and business life; and every one of practical experience knows that a large amount of the time consumed in a civil cause is taken up by reading and commenting on the correspondence. The speeches of counsel are no doubt longer than they used to be, but so, in the majority of instances, is the summing-up. One has only to compare the present-day reports with those of "Barnewall and Alderson," or "Meeson and Welsby," to see that a similar change has taken place in the judgments delivered by the judges. I cannot find anything in the Judicature Acts which accounts for this; and I believe that the real cause is to be looked for in the increased complexity of human affairs, rather than in any diminution in the conscientiousness or ability of the advocates. Whatever the cause may be, the effect upon the ordinary level of forensic oratory is undeniable. Few speakers can be entertaining for longer than a few minutes—or perhaps seconds. None can be consistently eloquent for more than half an hour. He, therefore, who is compelled to go on talking for a whole day cannot expect to give pleasure to anybody—except perhaps to his client. No advocate ever yet sat down without feeling convinced that he had at least done that—even if he has not pleased himself, as the worst speaker usually succeeds in doing.

One form of prolixity may be mentioned for which I think the advocate is not wholly responsible, if indeed he ever is (which I greatly doubt). I refer to the long-drawn arguments which take up so much time of the Court of Appeal. I do not know any member of the Bar who could argue for more than an hour about anything, if he were left severely alone, without any attempt being made by the Bench to convince him that he is wrong. The best illustration of my meaning is given by the well-worn story of the genial Chancery leader who was asked by the Court of Appeal if he had taken the point which he was arguing in the court below. "I did, my lord," was the reply, "but the learned judge stopped me." "How did he do that, Mr.

Blank?" inquired the President, with awakened interest. "By fraudulently pretending, my lord," said the indignant advocate, "that he was in my favour!" The other side of the picture, however, is vividly represented by the story told by a brilliant after-dinner speaker at the banquet given to the American Bar in the Middle Temple Hall some years ago. "Mr. Jones, Mr. Jones," said the wearied President of the United States Supreme Court, "you must give this court credit for knowing *something*." "That's all very well," replied the advocate (who came from a Western State), "but that's exactly the mistake I made in the court below!"

It may be that the prolixity of the arguments in the Court of Appeal has reacted upon the length of the judgments of that tribunal, which certainly sometimes extend to portentous length. A former President of the court was once delivering a judgment of this kind, when he was interrupted by the next Lord Justice, who mistook the end of a period for the final peroration. "I agree," said the interrupter, with incisive curtness. "But you have not yet heard my reasons," said the President, with a smile. The Lord

Justice bowed apologetically and listened attentively for another quarter of an hour. When the close really came he had his revenge. "I still agree!" was the form in which he thought fit to concur.

There is, however, one instance at least where the prolongation of the advocate's eloquence was of considerable service to his client. The American lawyer who defended Guiteau, the assassin of President Garfield, spoke for five days, with the object of delaying the conclusion of the trial, so as to postpone the execution of the prisoner until the end of the following term. The orator was so far successful that, though the trial took place in January, 1882, the sentence of death was not carried out until the ensuing July. One of the many curious incidents of this trial was, that the prisoner himself desired to address the jury before his counsel. This the judge refused to allow, on the ground that it was safe to assume that the prisoner would abuse the privilege. Whereupon the criminal sent the manuscript of his proposed speech to the Press, which appears to have published it in full! The substance of this effusion was a demand that an acquittal should be directed, on the ground that he was suffering from "transitory mania" when the President was shot, and so was "overpowered by the Deity!" So far as his speech was concerned, he got his own way after all, and was ultimately permitted to address the jury after his counsel had finished. It is noteworthy that the summing-up only occupied an hour and a half, and there can be little doubt that the advocate deliberately prolonged his speech to get the benefit of delay.

The longest civil trial on record is, I suppose, the Tichborne case, which occupied no less than a hundred and three days before the jury stopped it. My only personal recollection of that extraordinary performance is confined to one afternoon. I was a pupil in a pleader's chambers at the time, and strolled down to Westminster one day to see if I could get into the court. With the audacity of sheer ignorance, I made for the judge's entrance, facing Westminster Abbey. The policeman on duty called an inspector, to whom I explained my wishes. He ushered me with much deference through a number of corridors, till we reached a door shaded by a heavy baize curtain. Through this he motioned me to pass, which I did without any suspicion, and found myself on the Bench, about six feet from Bovill, C.J., who was trying the case. As there was a vacant chair, I thought I should be less conspicuous if I sat down, and I remained there undisturbed for the rest of the afternoon. My glory was shared by no one except a lady, whose eyes I carefully avoided meeting. The Chief Justice took no notice of either of us, and I wondered if she had any better title to be present than myself. The chair was undoubtedly placed for somebody, who fortunately failed to keep his appointment, or more probably was turned back as an impostor by my friend the inspector. My own theory at the time was that I had been mistaken for the Duke of Connaught, whom I was pleased at that age to think that I resembled. Had such a thing happened on circuit I should not have been surprised, as an assize judge seldom thinks of inquiring into the arrangements made by the under-sheriff; and I remember once seeing a lady of dubious virtue occupying a similar position, to the horror and amusement of the junior Bar. Neither the judge nor the sheriff suspected anything, and nobody at the end of the day seemed a penny the worse. Remembering my own adventure at Westminster, I kept sympathetic silence.

The civil court on circuit seldom produces any monstrosities in the way of length, though, by way of compensation, some of the cases are tried twice or even three times over. The best specimen of which I had personal experience was a Bodmin cause, which was not only thrice tried before a jury, but went twice to the House of Lords, and is enshrined in the Law Reports under the title of *Foxwell v. Van Grutten*. It turned ultimately upon the rule in Shelley's case (which the student under examination stated to be the same as in anybody else's case, as the law was no respecter of persons!). The judgment of Lord Macnaghten on the final appearance of this case in the House of Lords is probably the only instance in which this repulsive subject has been treated, not only with learning, but with literary skill, and even humour. The history of the case might well have furnished the plot for a novel, all the same. Nearly a century ago two old men named Harris died in Cornwall, leaving considerable wealth behind them. The money was, I believe, made out of tin-mining; though malicious people

H

were found to suggest that most of it had been acquired by driving a donkey about on the sea-cliffs with a lantern tied to its tail—in other words, by the nefarious practice of wrecking. The property descended to one Mary Harris, the daughter of one brother, the niece of the other. The heiress married a widower of better social position and less means than herself, and the ingenuity of the best conveyancers of that day was employed in an attempt to tie up her fortune so that the husband's family should never get hold of it. The marriage settlements and the wills were all miracles of conveyancing art ; but no lay-man or lawyer was ever able to understand their effect. The heiress lost her reason—perhaps in trying to comprehend them—after a separation from her husband, and lived to a great age—not unhappy, I trust, as she died under the belief that she was the Duchess of Cornwall. She left one son, who was also a lunatic, and survived his mother many years. During this prolonged period the estates were administered under the lunacy jurisdiction of the Court of Chancery. Upon the death of the lunatic, without issue, the fight for the property began. The contest was whether his heirs should inherit—which meant the descendants of his father (Mary's husband) *by his first wife*—or whether the heirs of the two old men (the original testators) were entitled. This question depended upon the proper construction of the wills and settlements, and of other deeds executed by Mary in her lifetime, some before she became insane and some afterwards. Moreover, it was very difficult to ascertain who the heirs of old William and Henry Harris were, and still more difficult to prove their pedigree when they were found. There were, indeed, many other complications, which would be of no interest to the general reader. The House of Lords ultimately decided the case in such a way that the bulk of the property went to the descendants of Mary Harris's husband by his first wife. During the final hearing the counsel for the other side, becoming very hard pressed, urged upon their lordships that a decision adverse to his clients would probably make the bones of all the Harrises turn in their graves. It is to be feared that this argument had little effect upon the tribunal, and it will be found that Lord Macnaghten's judgment is silent upon the point. The atmosphere of the House of

Lords is, indeed, not congenial to such considerations. It is, however, an illustration of the irony of fate, that the destination of a considerable property should have been determined in this way, through the slip of an ancient conveyancer made nearly a century ago.

The technicalities of real-property law are not lightly to be inflicted upon the reader, but one incident of the trial seems to me worth preserving. The judge who tried the case for the third time did not profess to be familiar with conveyancing, and during its progress asked one of the counsel to tell him the exact meaning of a " base fee." I have little doubt that the learned judge knew very well, and (alternatively) that he could have tried the cause quite satisfactorily without knowing. The counsel who was asked the question had not been put into the case to argue points of law, but he made a courageous attempt to reply. He answered that a base fee was a sort of branch line running parallel to the original line. This violation of a primary proposition of Euclid did not satisfy the judicial seeker after knowledge, and he appealed to a Chancery junior who had been brought down special in order to answer inconvenient questions of this character. The explanation given by this expert was, I am sure, quite correct; but I am bound to add that it was also unintelligible. Self-respect, however, sealed the judge's lips against any further investigation of the subject; and I often wonder if he knows now. So far as I remember, neither the question nor the answer had any bearing upon the trial which was proceeding at the time.

One more anecdote of this litigation may throw a sidelight upon some of the multifarious duties discharged by counsel. A very learned and conscientious junior had been briefed to " watch " the case, from Nisi Prius up to the House of Lords, on behalf of certain claimants who believed themselves to be interested in the result. At the luncheon interval, on the third or fourth day of the final hearing, the friendly solicitor who instructed him inquired in a stage whisper if he would like to be introduced "to the mug." "What mug ? " asked the barrister, a little perplexed. " Why, *the* mug," replied his candid client. " I mean the mug who's paying you to watch ! "

The only other case which I can recollect to

have been tried three times was an action
about the ownership of a hedge. As most
country people know, the presumption of law
is that the hedge belongs to the man on
whose side the ditch is not—the theory being
that the landowner digs a ditch on the extreme verge of his own property, and throws
up the earth on his own soil because he may
not trespass on his neighbour's. In this case
the ownership of the hedge involved the right
to the frontage for building purposes; and
both plaintiff and defendant wanted to prove
that a ditch had formerly existed on the one
side or the other. The first jury, if I
remember right, said that the ditch had been
on the side of the plaintiff; the second jury,
that it had been on the side of the defendant.
The third jury gave it as their opinion that
there never had been any ditch at all—and
this was probably true. The costs in this case
must have amounted to the fee-simple value
of the land several times over. Let not the
captious critic inquire how the Court of
Appeal came to permit a third trial. It may
have been that there was a disagreement of
the jury at the second attempt. Two things
I am, at any rate, certain about—that the case

was in fact tried three times; and that not even the blind man leading the blind could have tumbled into that ditch. Leading a most clear-sighted junior, I tried very hard to accomplish the feat myself, but without success.

.   .   .   .   .   .

The reluctance of the Court of Appeal to order a new trial, which has just been referred to, raises a very serious question. It is undeniable, of course, that new trials cost money, and are in that sense a misfortune to the litigants. The greatest misfortune, how-ever, that a litigant can suffer is injustice; and the Court of Appeal exists to prevent this from happening, and not for the purpose of saving his pocket. The question of finance is for the litigants themselves and their pro-fessional advisers, and for them alone. Every honest lawyer, whether solicitor or counsel, recognizes that it is his imperative duty to weigh carefully his client's position, and to dissuade him from running the risks of an appeal or a new trial, if he is not a man who can afford to take them. There are very few advocates who cannot recall dozens of cases in which they have reluctantly taken this course, even when they were convinced that the chances of success were good. Law, however, is not an exact science; and the cases are few and far between in which counsel can advise their clients that success on appeal is a certainty. At the best there is an element of gambling in all litigation; nor do I know why counsel should not adopt the notation of the book-maker to measure the risk involved. To tell a man that he has " a good fighting chance " or a " reasonable prospect of success " conveys no definite idea, for the words " good " and " reasonable " have not a fixed meaning. If he were told that in the opinion of his adviser the odds were two to one in his favour, or six to four against him, he would understand better where he stood. But it is his business, and that of his advisers, to decide whether he can afford to take a six-to-four chance—say, in hundreds; and the sole function of a court of justice is to see that he has a fair run for his money.

The first and most important qualification for an advocate, to enable him to advise on an appeal against the verdict of a jury on a question of fact, is to know the principle upon which the appeal will be decided by the court. In theory, the verdict of a jury ought to be set aside, if, and only if, that verdict is wrong. What does "wrong" mean? The only answer, I think, that can be given to this question is, that it must be wrong in the opinion of the court which hears the appeal. *Ex hypothesi*, it was right in the opinion of the jury who gave it, or it would not have been given; and it is difficult to find any logical ground for regarding the fact of its existence as a reason for considering it right when reviewed. There is a presumption, of course, in its favour; that is to say, the burden of attacking it lies on the appellant; but that is all. If the appellant presents such facts to the judges as to create in their minds the belief that the verdict is wrong, he ought to succeed. It cannot be necessary to show that it is more than wrong, or very wrong, or wrong with any other epithet. It is with unfeigned deference that I submit the next proposition. If the judges of the Appeal Court are satisfied that they would have found a different verdict, they must logically be of opinion that the verdict appealed against is wrong, and the appellant ought to succeed. Further, it is their province to decide mentally, aye or no, are they satisfied that they would have found a different verdict ; and not to stop half-way at the point where they are not satisfied that they would have found the same one. It goes without saying that if their conviction is not strong enough to carry them past that point the appellant has not made out his case. All that I am contending for is that the appellant is entitled to call upon them to go further, if they can.

It may be useful at this point—and not, I hope, presumptuous—to consider a form of phraseology which has not unfrequently been heard of late years in the Court of Appeal. It is said that the question is not whether the judges of appeal agree with the verdict, but whether the verdict is such that twelve reasonable men could not have found it. This sounds like a mathematical formula, but I do not think it can be defended as such. The word " twelve " is surely immaterial, and may be eliminated. Many cases are tried by consent with a jury of eleven or even less, and in the County Courts the number of jurors is five. To say that a verdict is such that it could not have been arrived at by reasonable men is only another way of expressing that it is in conflict with the reason of the speaker —that is to say, that he disagrees with it very strongly. If he disagrees with it in such a sense that he would have found a different verdict himself, can it logically be said that any stronger disagreement is necessary ? The word " disagree " is perhaps itself ambiguous. It may be used either to signify that the speaker does not affirmatively agree, or that he negatively dissents and differs. When the first meaning is intended, and only the first meaning, it has been conceded above that the appeal has not been supported. But if it is used with the second meaning, the mind that in that sense disagrees with a verdict must consider it to be wrong. And if it be wrong, can it matter *how* wrong ? Surely all men are to be regarded as reasonable—until our own reason disagrees with them ; but no longer.

The fact that a jury have the advantage of seeing the faces and observing the demeanour of the witnesses, is justly entitled to great weight ; but it does not affect the present argument. Its natural operation is to retard any disagreement with their verdict ; but it ought not to alter or modify the *effect* of that disagreement when once fairly reached. This is obvious enough; but it should also be remembered that it is for this very reason that a Court of Appeal, in an ordinary case, does not itself pronounce the verdict which it thinks ought to be given, but is contented to order a new trial. Cases where judgment is directed in opposition to a verdict are exceptional. The sanctity of trial by jury, so far as criminal cases are concerned, is not likely to be violated; but I cannot help thinking that with respect to civil litigation it has become something of a fetish. Certainly there is a marked difference between the respect—I had almost written the reverence—paid to it by the Court of Appeal and the practical appreciation of its advantages that is shown by the Bar. It has become almost a commonplace duty for counsel, in cases where he feels his client is wrong, to advise trial before a jury. It is true that he often gives the same advice when his case is a good one; but usually only with the object of getting inflated damages—that is to say, more than his client deserves. I do not in the least suggest that such advice is improper; but it is this practice which renders it possible for a County Court judge to speak as one is reported to have done the other day. According to the newspaper report, his experience was, "that if it was possible for a jury to do wrong they would invariably do it ; and that if people had a rotten action they asked for a jury, knowing that they would probably get what a judge would not give them." It is impossible for me to conjecture what is the mental attitude on this subject of the High Court judges who try the cases ; but I do know what is their actual practice. With hardly an exception, it is the habit of the judge in summing-up to express his own opinion on the facts as strongly as possible, and while deferring to principle by telling the jury that the decision must be theirs, to tell them indirectly—sometimes directly—what he thinks that decision ought to be. I am far from suggesting that this practice is not beneficial to the interests of justice. On the contrary, I think it is ; but why is it necessary ? The answer which most men will give is, because juries are not to be trusted to do justice if left to themselves. In the large majority of cases juries follow the guidance of the judge, and are thankful to have him to lean on. Sometimes—but comparatively seldom—they find against his direction. If this is true, it follows that in

a large number of cases the verdict appealed
against is not the verdict of twelve laymen,
but of one lawyer. I do not mean that the
jurors have not tried to exercise their own
judgment, but that they would just as readily
have found a verdict the other way if the
judge had so advised them. I once heard a
judge conclude his summing-up to a jury as
follows: " I dare say you will have gathered
from what I have said that I think you
ought to find for the defendant. *So I do;*
and I further think that you will be very
wrong if you don't." It will be said that this
must have been an extreme case. That must
always be a matter of opinion ; but I am quite
sure that the learned judge in that instance
could have obtained a verdict for the plaintiff
just as easily as he did for the defendant ; and
this is true of the large majority of cases tried.
If it is important—as I believe it to be—to
try to prevent a jury from going wrong, surely
it is at least as important to remedy the wrong
when they have done it ?   Is there any reason
why a jury should be permitted, so to speak,
a margin of error, allowed to go wrong, but
not outrageously wrong ? And if the opinion
of one judge of first instance is rightly used

to obtain a verdict on an issue of fact, surely the opinion of three judges of appeal on the same material should be sufficient to set it aside. The Court of Appeal has, of course, a most difficult duty to perform, and to say that they fill their high position so as to command the admiration of the civilized world is so true that it sounds almost impertinent.   But it is none the less certain that under the present system many unrighteous or mistaken verdicts are permitted to stand ; and the sense of injustice never presses more heavily on the disappointed litigant than when he has appealed against such a verdict in vain.

CHAPTER V

THE CRIMINAL COURT

THE Criminal Court is not always a place of gloom, and the crowd which invariably besieges its portals testifies to the superiority of its attractions over those of Nisi Prius. The veteran advocate himself, in the majority of cases, recalls his performances in that arena with fond complacency rather than remorse ; and is usually prouder of the acquittals he has obtained in the teeth of justice, than of all the other harm he may have done in a long lifetime. It is there that the newly fledged barrister, either as a prosecutor or defender of small criminals, looks for his first opportunity of distinction, at an age when both the glow of success and the mortification of defeat are felt most keenly. Not until the maturity of age has knocked most of his ideals on the head does he turn for real interest to a building contract, and learn to quench his passions in a rating appeal. There

are great judges who have risen to the Bench
without any such adventurings, but it is
generally admitted that they have missed
something of the joy of life.

Most advocates of any experience are frequently asked by the curious whether they
have ever seen an innocent man convicted.
To say that they had never seen an innocent
man tried would savour of frivolity, but in
most cases it would be as near the truth as
any other answer they could give.   Now that
a court for criminal appeals has been duly
constituted, it is of course necessary that it
should justify its own existence, and doubtless there are many prisoners tried who ought
to be acquitted.   Many there are of whom
the jury are rightly directed that they ought
to say "Not Guilty," and many more of
whom juries say the same when they ought
not; but the white flower of innocence is a
rare plant, and seldom blooms in the dock.
It is not uncharitable to say that cases in
which acquittal means that the charge has
been disproved, and that the judge is as satisfied of the prisoner's innocence as of his own,
are not of frequent occurrence.   The jurymen
may sometimes be so satisfied, for aught that

any one else can tell; but of course their standard of innocence is not so high; and it must be remembered that juries are often misled by the evidence—sometimes, indeed, by the summing-up.

The public, I think, are hardly aware that in the majority of criminal cases—it may be said, without exaggeration, in all capital ones —everybody in court, judge, jury, witnesses, and counsel included, is engaged in a tacit and merciful conspiracy to get the prisoner off—if it can be done with decency. Taking a plea of guilty on a charge of murder is indeed regarded as unsportsmanlike as shooting a fox—or perhaps chopping one in covert. This is in deference to what is known as "the spirit of English law"; but indeed I think that this spirit is quite a modern one, and that things were very different little more than half a century ago. The modern spirit, however, reigned supreme until the recent alteration in the law, which enabled prisoners to give evidence on their own behalf. Inasmuch as this innovation unquestionably increased the chances of conviction for the guilty, it might almost be described as a retrograde step. As an indirect consequence, it became necessary to pass the

Poor Prisoners' Defence Act; in order that every criminal who is invited by the judge to submit himself for cross-examination by the prosecuting counsel, may have at his side a professional adviser to caution him against doing so. "I guess, judge, I'll remain neutral," is the wise answer attributed to a negro prisoner in America, who was asked by the judge whether or not he desired to take the witness-chair. That he may follow this advice without embarrassment, the benevolence of the law prohibits the advocate for the Crown from criticizing his silence; so that, after all, he is not much worse off than he used to be. Even an innocent man knows that his counsel can certainly invent a better defence for him than he could for himself, and it is common knowledge that "instructions for the defence" too often consist of an inadequate endorsement on the back of a copy of the depositions. The solicitor in such cases either knows too much or imparts too little—sometimes, indeed, he does both.

The theory of English law, and the only logical one, is that in order to justify a conviction, the evidence must exclude the fair possibility of any other hypothesis than that of guilt. In other words, if any state of facts can be suggested which is consistent with the evidence, and also with the innocence of the prisoner, there ought to be an acquittal. It follows that possibility, and not truth, is the essential element of a defence; and though a theory which is probable as well as possible is none the worse on that account, it is no more necessary, logically speaking, that it should be probable than that it should be true. If it can be shown to be demonstrably untrue, it ceases to be consistent with the evidence, and therefore ceases to be possible as an explanation. The advocate is then driven to the contention that the evidence with which it is in conflict is untrue, and that the hypothetical defence is accordingly still a possible one. But even in this extremity it is unnecessary, and often dangerous, to allege that it is true. Only when the prisoner is telling his own story, either in the witness-box or from the dock, is the hypothetical defence at a disadvantage. The jury are not so foolish as to expect him to tell them the truth, but they cannot help suspecting that he is able to do so.

The result of these well-worn truisms is

that defences in the Criminal Court usually
assume one of two typical forms. The
advocate has either to explain away the
evidence or to deny the veracity of the
witnesses. If he has to do both, the prisoner
is usually in a parlous state. There is, however, a third line of defence, not always to
be ventured upon, but sometimes successful
enough before a Cornish jury, and very
popular on the other side of the English
Channel. It consists in persuading the jurors
that it would be a greater crime for them to
convict the prisoner than it was for him to
deserve conviction. Of this method the
American appeal to the " unwritten law " is
a sort of glorified example ; but illustrations
are often to be found nearer home. Some
years ago I remember witnessing the prosecution of a scoundrel popularly known as " Dr.
Jack," who was tried at Bodmin for murder
resulting from an illegal operation. The
excellent and amiable judge who tried the
case summed up with judicial clearness for
a conviction, but he was ignorant of some
very pertinent facts. He did not know that
the prisoner had inherited his nefarious business from his father, that he was regarded

I 2

in the neighbourhood as a public benefactor rather than a criminal, and that arrangements had already been made to meet him at the railway-station, in the event of an acquittal, with a carriage and a brass band. The jury listened to the summing-up with resolute indifference, with the result that the carriage proved not to have been ordered in vain, and the band played. It is pleasant to add that the prisoner was convicted afterwards in London of a similar offence, for which he received ten years' penal servitude.

I do not suggest that Cornish juries, on an average, are worse than those in other counties; but certainly they have earned a unique reputation for what may be euphemistically called independence. Cornish prisoners often exhibit something of the same quality. As an illustration, I remember the trial of a perfectly respectable farmer in that county, who one morning found a man lying asleep under his hayrick. The farmer called to him three times to get up, threatening to knock him on the head if he did not obey, but the poor wretch was too besotted with drink to answer. Thereupon the owner of the rick, who had in his hand a heavy potato-hoe, incontinently and without more ado smashed the trespasser's skull into a pulp. The jury, in this case, plainly wanted to acquit the prisoner altogether, and were with difficulty persuaded by the judge to return a verdict of manslaughter. But they appended a strong recommendation to mercy, on the ground of " extreme provocation "! Perhaps an agricultural jury may be forgiven for regarding the conjunction of a tramp and a hayrick as an unpleasant one.

Cases of this description defend themselves; but in capital cases which appeal less powerfully to the imagination, the defending advocate has usually full scope for his ingenuity, and the most audacious theories are often put forward with success. The jury are overweighted with a sense of responsibility, and will swallow almost any excuse for an acquittal, however artificial, if artistically presented. The prisoner's counsel is allowed almost unlimited indulgence, and though I do not say—or think—that it is often abused, he certainly takes the fullest advantage of his privileges. On the other hand, the position of the prosecutor is a very difficult one, and he is constantly distracted between a desire to be fair and temperate, and his primary obligation to see that justice is not evaded. The judge seldom feels it his duty to make any strong effort for a conviction in a capital case; and where the prosecution is in weak hands the verdict often goes wrong. No doubt it is well that it should be so. The errors of a merciful system of jurisprudence are not always to be deplored; and if justice were infallible the black cap might properly be assumed by the committing magistrate.

Of those trials for murder which I have witnessed on circuit, the most vivid impression has been left on my memory by a case which was heard at Bristol in the early eighties. The prisoner—who shall be left nameless—was indicted for the murder of his wife. He was by occupation a labourer at the gasworks, and on Saturday afternoons was accustomed to vary the monotony of his calling by assisting a neighbouring butcher to slaughter sheep. He lived with his wife and four or five children in a wretched tenement near his work, and between ten and eleven o'clock one night a doctor was called in by some of the neighbours, who found the woman lying dead in bed. She had, in fact, been stabbed in the back with a sharp knife, and the evidence conclusively showed that her husband was in the room with her at the time, and that no stranger could possibly have entered or left the dwelling. There was some evidence of a previous quarrel, and there had certainly been a determined attempt to conceal the tragedy. An old woman was tried and convicted at the same assize of being an accessory after the fact, and was sentenced, if I remember right, to a year's imprisonment. The medical man who was called in was not told, and did not for some time detect, that anything unusual had taken place. He assumed from what he was told that the woman had died from heart disease ; and, indeed, the only object with which he was called in was to induce him to certify to this effect. In all probability he would have done so ; but just as he was about to leave the room something excited a misgiving, and he hastily turned back the bedclothes. So nearly did the audacious attempt at concealment attain success !

The defence which had been foreshadowed before the committing justices was that the wound was either the result of an accident or had been self-inflicted. To meet this contention the prosecution obtained from the hospital a dummy life-size model or body, on which the course of the wound—which had passed from the back through the lungs—was clearly indicated in red. The defence actually set up at the trial was that of misadventure, which was explained in the following way. It was said that the woman, after going to bed, sent for her supper of bread and cheese; and ate it in bed, leaning on her right elbow. That she placed or dropped the knife behind her with her left hand, in such a manner that it stuck more or less upright; and that when she had finished eating she threw herself backwards, forgetting the knife, and was impaled upon it by her own weight. To show the possibility of such an accident, the actual bed and bedding, with the fatal knife, were brought into court, and a witness made experiments with them before the eyes of the jury. As a spectator, I was not myself impressed with the demonstration. Some people, however, were so impressed—or persuaded themselves that they were; and if there had been nothing more in the case, it is possible that the jury might have accepted the suggestion. No one, certainly, could have shown more ingenuity or determination in presenting this theory than the prisoner's advocate (C. W. Mathews), who made a great effort for the defence.

It was necessary for the Crown to call as witnesses the four children of the unhappy couple, who were certainly present in the room when the material events happened. They all professed to have seen nothing. The eldest, a boy of fifteen or sixteen, said that he was on his knees saying his prayers, when he heard a groan, and looked up to see his mother lying back in her last agony. There was a little girl about ten years old, whose examination was the most painful part of the whole proceeding. The poor child was suffering from a form of rupture, of which fact no one was aware; and the ordeal of giving evidence brought on such physical distress that the trial had to be twice suspended in order to allow her to recover. Eventually a doctor was called in, who discovered what was wrong; and after the little sufferer had been fitted with a truss, her examination was concluded. Repeated appeals were made to the prosecution to dispense with her evidence; but it would have been risking too much to allow the defence such a topic for suggestion to the jury; and the other course was taken, with the approval of the judge. This child had, in fact, been sent out to buy the bread and cheese which the woman was supposed to have been eating. Her evidence, as given in court, was that nothing was wrong with her mother at the time when she was sent out; but it was known to the prosecution, and doubtless also to the defence, that the child had stated to the shopkeeper that her mother was very ill. The rules of evidence did not allow the prosecution to prove this, or to cross-examine the child as to her having said it. If the judge had known as much as the prosecution, it may be that he would have asked the question; but it did not appear on the depositions. There can be no doubt that the woman was either dead or dying when the child was sent out; and the purchase was part of the scheme to conceal what had taken place, concocted between the prisoner and the old woman who was convicted as an accessory.

The jury found the prisoner guilty after a trial which occupied three long days, and he duly suffered the penalty of his crime. There was, of course, a petition; and it was stated that on the day before the execution a telegram was sent to the Home Secretary in the name of the eldest son, saying that his evidence at the trial had been untrue, and that he could prove what actually happened if a reprieve were granted. If such a telegram was sent it failed in its object, and the law was allowed to take its course.

The interest in such cases usually dies out when the execution of the criminal is an accomplished fact, but in this instance the question was retried in the Press over and over again. Considerable ingenuity was shown by amateur correspondents in suggesting defences which might have been adopted in lieu of that which failed. One only of these is worth reproduction, which formed the subject of a long article in a monthly magazine, and appeared some weeks after the sentence of the law had been carried out. The writer, after detailing some of the facts which had been narrated, called attention to the point that the fatal knife was the same as that which the criminal was accustomed to use on Saturday afternoons, when he served as assistant to a butcher. (He might have added with truth, if he had known the fact, that it was the only knife on the premises, and was used for all household purposes indiscriminately.) The theory he propounded was that the knife had been carelessly left in the bed after the woman had eaten her supper; that the man had then gone to bed and fallen asleep; that as he slept, his hand accidentally came into contact with the knife; that the accustomed feel of the handle suggested to his dreaming brain that he was killing a sheep; and that he thereupon instinctively carried out the suggestion by stabbing his wife! Somnambulism could hardly go further than that. Most people will agree that to have put forward such a theory at the trial would have been a deplorable error. Ridicule is the most fatal enemy of the advocate.

As an incident of this case, I may mention that it was tried in the hottest week of a hot summer, and that the thermometer which hung over the head of the clerk of assize indicated well over 90° on three successive afternoons. This temperature Sir Henry Hawkins seemed hugely to enjoy, sitting until nine o'clock or thereabouts on each day with perfect contentment. The gallery was crowded with spectators; and the learned judge had an invincible objection to any door being open for the fraction of a second. About five o'clock on the hottest of the three days he gave private instructions to his clerk, and the key was shortly afterwards heard to turn in the gallery door. It was not opened again until the court rose, three hours and a half later.

Few people had a more inveterate objection to fresh air than Sir Henry Hawkins, who at one time had a sort of movable sentry-box constructed for his use in court, in order to prevent the possibility of a draught. He once explained his preference for suffocation to chill on the ground that it was a "slower death." Mr. Baron Huddleston had the same peculiarity, and was accustomed on occasion to direct not only that every window should be closed, but that the sashes should be pasted down with paper. To pass from one of these infernos on circuit into the other court, where some judge like Mr. Justice Wills might be presiding with the four winds of heaven searching every corner, was an experience not to be forgotten.

Another capital case from the Western
Circuit, memorable for a far-fetched but successful defence, came from the county of
Wilts, and was tried at Winchester during
the period when the system of "grouped
assizes" was in operation in the spring of
1886. A small baker in a quiet country town
was charged with poisoning his wife. The
couple were miserably poor and lived on
unhappy terms enough, but there was no
evidence of any particular quarrel between
them. The woman died suddenly, and the
post-mortem examination disclosed that she
had swallowed both arsenic and strychnine in
sufficient quantities to kill half a dozen men.
Her husband had been for a time an assistant
in a chemist's shop, and there was evidence
which showed that he could have obtained
the drugs without much difficulty. There
were many facts which raised a strong suspicion against him, and though there was
nothing conclusive a strong circumstantial
case was made out. They lived alone with
two young children, and the main difficulty
for the defence was to suggest any hypothesis
which would account for the presence of the
arsenic and strychnine in the woman's stomach.

The theory successfully put forward was that the woman had voluntarily taken both drugs, not with any idea of suicide, but under the belief that she was again *enceinte*, and that these rather violent measures were likely to produce abortion. There was some slight evidence that she had expressed her dread of again becoming a mother, and so adding to the labours and privations of her already burdened existence. The main difficulty, however, was to persuade the jury that it was possible for a woman—especially a married woman—to resort to such desperate expedients for such a reason. The medical man who knew most of the woman's history was fortunately able to declare his belief in the possibility of what certainly seemed very improbable, and was in a position to support his view by a long medical experience in a rural district. I remember his telling the jury, amongst other things, that the ignorance of women in the lower classes on this subject was amazing, and that he had himself known a case where a girl took a whole packet of Batty's vermin-killer with the same object, and survived the experiment. He was careful to add that it did not even have the

K

desired effect, being doubtless anxious lest the prescription he was thus making public should become too popular. The jury did not like to convict the man in the face of this theory, and certainly it was not a case in which a conviction would have been regarded by anybody with unmixed feelings. The woman indeed might have committed suicide, for aught either counsel or any one else in the case knew. A singular situation would have been created if it had been shown that she happened to take strychnine for one purpose on the same day that she was given arsenic for another. The jury might then have had to decide whether the first poison was rapid enough in its operation to anticipate the effect of the second. Fortunately their task was not so complex.

It has always appeared to me a curious freak of taste which leads so many people to devote their attention to the rare cases of wrongful conviction, while the great number of instances in which the guilty escape scot free excite little, if any interest. *Judex damnatur cum nocens absolvitur* is a maxim which, of course, applies only to jurors, and no one would be so profane as to apply such language to a judge of the High Court, even in the Latin tongue. Statistics are not an attractive subject; still, a great number of respectable people would be astonished if they knew how large a percentage of the acquittals in capital cases were undeserved. There was one member of the Bar, when I first entered the profession, who had for many years been the fortunate recipient of Treasury briefs. It was popularly said that he had enjoyed an unbroken sequence of twenty-nine successive acquittals in cases of murder, which must be an easy record, if true. The probabilities are that these figures included all the cases in which the capital sentence was escaped, either through a verdict of manslaughter only or by the intervention of the Home Secretary; but even so, the performance was a notable one.

Still, there can be few circuit tramps who do not recall some instances in which a sense that justice had not been vindicated remained long after the verdict, even in the minds of the least bloodthirsty. One case, in which I held a junior brief for the prosecution, many years ago, has never faded from my memory. The victim—unquestionably murdered by some-body—was a girl about sixteen years old, whose body was found in a field-pond, used as a watering-place for cattle. Death had taken place at least a fortnight before. She had lived in a cottage a few hundred yards away with her father and stepmother, whose drudge she had been for a considerable time. Her skull had been smashed in with some heavy instrument like an iron bar; and there were some indications that the body had been dragged up an overgrown path or lane to the place where it was concealed. Her father and stepmother, who had said nothing about her disappearance, were indicted for the murder. They were defended by a most competent advocate, to whom they undoubtedly owed their lives, and who directed his efforts to showing that there was another person who might conceivably have been guilty of the crime. There was not the slightest ground for any such imputation against him, and the defence seemed to me at the time dangerously near the border-line of fairness; but cooler reflection afterwards convinced me that the first duty of the advocate, in such a case, was rightly discharged. The person attacked was, in fact, so absolutely free from blame that the temporary imputation did him no harm, while it certainly saved the prisoners from the gallows. Popular feeling afterwards, however, was so strong that they left that part of the country; and the accursed cottage, for which no tenant could be found, was pulled down by the landlord. I remember one incident in the course of the case which caused a sensation in the court. The son of the prisoners, a boy of about nine years old, was giving evidence, and he spoke in his examination-in-chief of a large wooden box which was kept on the landing of the cottage. In cross-examination he was asked if he had ever seen it opened, and he said he had on one occasion. "What was in it?" asked the prisoner's counsel. "Bones!" was the unexpected and somewhat ghastly reply. The advocate's face was a study, and that line of cross-examination was not continued.

Home Secretaries and "mad doctors" between them save nearly as many lives as juries. In theory they are right enough; the cold-blooded murder, as distinguished from the sudden act of passion, is almost always indicative of an abnormal mental state. Yet it may be doubted if the commutation of the capital sentence is always the truest mercy—

it may not always be the most welcome. I remember one man whom I prosecuted for killing his wife. He was a one-armed man, and had been in the army, living at the time of the tragedy on a small pension and his wife's earnings as a charwoman. She was a middle-aged, hard-working woman of whom all the neighbours spoke well; but the man professed to be jealous of her, and they occupied separate rooms. One night he got up in the dark hours, went downstairs to his wife's room, and battered in her head with a hatchet. When he had made sure that she was dead, he made his way to the railway, and threw himself in front of a passing train. By some extraordinary chance he was not killed, but the train cut off his one remaining arm. The defence of insanity was set up, but did not succeed, and he was sentenced to death. His sentence was, however, commuted; and for aught I know, he may still be hanging out a maimed and miserable existence in Broadmoor. I was told that when lying under sentence of death he was visited by a doctor and the chaplain. He was, of course, strictly watched, and his armless condition required the presence of a prison warder in the cell with him day and night. This man happened to make a remark in answer to something said by the chaplain, whereon the murderer turned fiercely on him. " Shut up, you ——" he said. " You're only here to blow my nose, and d——d badly you do it!" Every one must recognize that the Home Secretary had no option but to commute the sentence, if the medical experts assured him that the man was insane. Yet is it possible to regard the prolongation of such a life as this as anything but a misfortune, as much to the man himself as to his fellow-creatures?

Of the four illustrative examples I have selected, it will be seen that three are cases of wife-murder. That is no doubt the commonest type; and next in frequency come, I think, murders by men of their sweethearts—if that word can be used in such a connection. Cases of this class usually resemble each other so closely that it seems not worth while recapitulating the facts of any particular instance. There is no doubt, however, that the number of murders due to perverted sexual passion—*crimes passionels*, as the French call them—is very large. Child-murder, too, is a common offence; and few

circuits pass over the rural districts without
two or three cases. Very often they are—or
were before the Poor Prisoners' Defence Act
—defended by some young barrister at the
request of the judge. Some of the older
judges were in the habit of paying the advocate a fee of two guineas from their own purse
in acknowledgment of this service. Hardly
ever does it happen that a woman convicted
of this offence suffers the capital penalty. The
jury acquit her, if possible, or find a verdict of
manslaughter, or concealment of birth—anything but wilful murder. In the rare cases
where the jury are compelled to convict, the
commutation of the sentence follows almost
as a matter of course. I think the authoress
of *Adam Bede* took an exaggerated view of
the severity of the law. In real life the peril
of Hetty Sorel would not have been great.
It was in a case of this kind that a Western
Circuit advocate once earnestly reminded the
jury that " even the beasts of the field and the
birds of the air suckle their young." " If you
can establish the truth of that proposition,
Mr. A.," said the learned judge, " you may
confidently look for an acquittal ! "

The strangest of all capital trials within the

writer's recollection was the celebrated *Mignonette* case; where the prisoners were charged with murder and cannibalism under the stress of shipwreck. I forget the exact ground upon which they escaped execution; but I do remember that it was proposed to entertain them at a public dinner, either at Portsmouth or Southampton, to celebrate their restoration to freedom. Some cynic, however, pointed out that there might be a difficulty about the *menu*, and the breath of ridicule happily put an end to the project. Another case which is still remembered is that of Lee, the Babbacombe murderer. He was a footman, convicted of murdering his mistress, an old lady who lived in a seaside cottage in one of the most lovely bays of South Devon. I heard him sentenced without realizing that there was anything exceptional about the case. Nor was there, except that it proved impossible to carry the sentence into effect. The "drop" upon which he stood, pinioned and blindfolded, would not fall, though three several attempts were made by the hangman to complete his task. Then the under-sheriff stopped the proceedings and telegraphed to the Home Office for instructions. In the result, the sentence was commuted to penal servitude for life. All sorts of stories were current in Devonshire at the time. It was said that the criminal was the natural son of some great man; and I am afraid that the name of more than one former light of the Western Circuit was profaned in this connection. The hangman was supposed to have been bribed, and whispers were heard of the complicity of the sheriff and the governor of the prison. It was gravely asserted—and the story was even repeated in the Press—that a white dove had been seen flying round the prison all the morning. The prosaic truth, I believe, was that some of the woodwork was unseasoned, and swollen with the wet, so that the drop jammed as soon as the man's weight was thrown upon it. That, at any rate, was the explanation given to me long afterwards by one of the officials of the gaol. Public interest was reawakened in this case a year or two ago by the discharge of the prisoner, after undergoing penal servitude for more than twenty years. His experiences got into the hands of the Press and were published by instalments in a weekly paper. The only comment to be made upon them is, that even the biography of a lawyer could hardly have been less interesting.

.   .   .   .   .   .

The disagreement of a jury in a capital case, though not an uncommon incident, is always an unfortunate one. It usually signifies two things: first, that the prisoner is guilty; and secondly, that he will never be convicted. Jurymen who know that one jury has already refused to find a verdict of guilty are very reluctant to accept the responsibility of doing so themselves. The Peasenhall case was tried three times, the result being two disagreements and an acquittal. Only a year or two ago a woman was tried for murder at Salisbury. The jury disagreed, but it was stated on good authority that there were eleven to one for a conviction. She was tried again at the next assizes, counsel for the prosecution and the defence being the same as before, and the jury acquitted her altogether after ten minutes' deliberation. What passed in the jury-room may easily be conjectured; but the secrets of that cheerless sanctum are sometimes jealously guarded, and when anything leaks out it is usually through the jury-bailiff. Tradition says that in the wilds of Cornwall that official was once sworn by a clerk who had mislaid the form of oath and endeavoured to repeat it from memory.

Taken down by an enterprising junior, it ran as follows : " You shall keep this jury in some private inconvenient place, without meat, drink, fire, or clothing. You shall not suffer them to speak to one another, neither shall you speak to them yourself, except to tell them what their verdict should be. So help you God ! " The truth of this story is not guaranteed ; but I am sure that it might easily have happened without any one noticing the variations from the correct version—just as I once heard a sheriff's chaplain include the judge's marshal in the " bidding prayer " at the cathedral without incurring any ecclesiastical censure.

.   .   .   .   .   .

It has been gravely asserted by a professional philosopher that morality is a fluid, incapable of congelation in mundane temperature, and entitled as of right to its natural flow. Evidence in support of this theory has indeed been adduced before a Parliamentary Committee on the question of the Censorship ; and if we are entitled to assume its truth, I see no reason why we should not regard criminality as the same fluid reduced

to the rarer condition of a gas. Distilled
immorality will on this assumption become
criminal, and only so long as it retains its non-
vaporous form will it remain immune. This
hypothesis has the merit of offering some
explanation of the difficulty so often ex-
perienced in the criminal courts of distinguishing between the two, the legal tests for the
purpose being indeed somewhat uncertain
and inconclusive. The advocate is thus too
often found impressing upon the jury the
immorality of his client, in the hope of
exciting rather their sympathy than their
censure ; while the judge has to struggle
against the instinctive desire of all really
good men to condemn the morality of other
people. In the long run and in the great
majority of cases, the result of this conflict
is greatly to the advantage of the prisoner ;
but on rare occasions a contrary effect has
been produced. The most classical instance,
perhaps, is the conviction of Alice Rhodes
for murder, in the case which many who are
still middle-aged will remember as the "Penge
Mystery." Two brothers named Staunton
were tried before Sir Henry Hawkins for the
murder by neglect and starvation of the

wife of the elder brother, and the girl Alice Rhodes, who was living with the husband of the dead woman, was included in the indictment. The unfortunate victim was weak both in mind and body; and until the day before her death was living in the house of the younger brother and his wife, who was the sister of Alice Rhodes. Except that the girl was the paramour of the guilty husband, and no doubt shared his strong desire for the death of the wife, it is difficult to see what there was against her. The deceased woman was not under her care or charge; and the most that can be said is that with knowledge of what was going on she abstained from interference. All the prisoners were convicted, but the Home Secretary intervened, and the girl ultimately received a free pardon, while the sentences upon the two brothers were commuted to penal servitude. It is not unlikely that the popular impression of Sir Henry Hawkins as a severe judge had its origin in this somewhat unfortunate case. The general opinion of the Bar, I believe, was that no judge ever took more anxious care to temper justice with mercy than the eminent criminal lawyer who was known to the younger generation as Lord Brampton. In his later years upon the bench he contracted the habit of deferring all his decisions at assizes until the last available day, when he was accustomed to occupy an unconscionable amount of time in passing sentence upon one prisoner after another with extreme deliberation. It would not be difficult to find arguments either in favour of this practice—or against it. Circuit reformers of to-day, however, would not find their difficulties lessened if his example were generally followed.

There can, I think, be little doubt that charges of murder by poison affect the popular imagination more strongly than any others, probably because in such cases it is easier for the ordinary man to identify himself with the victim—or with the criminal. Most of us are too highly civilized for crimes of violence, and are conscious that if it came to actual bloodshed we should lack the necessary moral courage, as did Macbeth. But the biggest coward of us all feels that, if the necessity arose, he might have sufficient nerve to dissolve a few crystals in his wife's tea. Borgia, Brinvilliers, Palmer, and Madeline Smith are therefore more attractive personalities than Thurtell,

Lefroy, Cain, or Jack the Giant-killer, though one of the latter had, at any rate, the charm of originality, and another is adorned with all the glamour of fiction. The most interesting trial of this kind to which I ever listened was the Lamson case in 1882, memorable as the last capital case in which Montagu Williams appeared for the defence. The interest of this case arose mainly from the fact that the poison which was administered to the victim was a rare vegetable alkaloid, called aconitine. Aconitine is the essential principle or alkaloid of aconite or monkshood, and almost defies detection by analysis, upon which fact the prisoner confidently relied. The crime in this case was brought home, not by any skill of the advocate, but rather (as it appeared to me) by the courageous and scientific hardihood of the expert witnesses. It was proved beyond doubt that death had resulted from the presence of *some* vegetable alkaloid in the system, but there was no test known by which the special alkaloid could be identified except by the sense of *taste*. The Treasury expert (Dr. Stevenson) after explaining how an alkaloidal extract had been prepared from the contents of the stomach of the victim, described the experiment he had made in the following language: "It produced, when placed on the tongue, a burning sensation which extended to the lip, though the extract did not touch the lip. The character of the sensation was a burning—a tingling—a sense of numbness. It is difficult to describe. It produced a salivation, creating a desire to expectorate, and a sensation at the back of the throat as if it were swelling up; and this was followed by a peculiar seared feeling, as if a hot iron had been drawn over the tongue, or something caustic placed upon it. . . . The sensation on the tongue lasted for four hours." (!)

The same witness, and also the Government analyst (Mr. Dupré) went on to say that a similar extract, prepared from the vomit of the victim, produced sensations of the same kind which lasted six hours and a half! When it is remembered that these scientific witnesses explained that the quantity of aconitine sufficient to kill an adult was somewhere between one-thirteenth and one-twenty-fourth part of a grain, the enterprise of those who conducted these repulsive and dangerous experiments will be better appre-

L

ciated—to say nothing of the additional tasting experiments with undoubted and unpolluted aconitine which were necessary for the purpose of identification. It was suggested for the defence that alkaloids of a somewhat similar nature, called "cadaveric alkaloids," are often spontaneously generated in decomposing bodies, and I forget how many tastings of a like nature had been made with all sorts of horrors for the purpose of refuting this suggestion. Let the advocate, who sometimes regards his fees as incommensurate with his merits, reflect what sort of money inducement would be sufficient to persuade him to do the like. Nothing but the highest sense of professional duty would be an adequate motive for such an undertaking, and though Sir Farrer Herschell, then Solicitor-General, conducted the prosecution on behalf of the Crown, I do not hesitate to say that the main factor in the vindication of justice was the self-devotion of the expert witnesses, Dr. Stevenson and Mr. Dupré.

One more sensational case of the same class to which I listened at the Old Bailey a few years later made a great impression on the public mind—the trial of Adelaide Bartlett

for the alleged murder of her husband. She
was charged with having poisoned him by
the administration of chloroform in its fluid
form, and much of the popular interest in
the case arose from the fact that a young
clergyman was originally included in the
indictment and was afterwards called as a
witness by the Crown. Two circumstances
made the case memorable in my mind. The
first was that the prisoner was defended by
the present Sir Edward Clarke, whose address
to the jury was perhaps the most brilliant
achievement of all his brilliant career, and
obtained the success which it deserved. The
other circumstance was that a witness was
recalled, after the speech for the defence was
over and the case closed except for the summing-up, to be asked an apparently harmless
and unimportant question. Unfortunately,
the witness gave an answer of a most serious
and damaging kind, having a grave bearing
upon the marital relations between the
prisoner and the dead man. I think it added
greatly to the difficulty which the judge (Mr.
Justice Wills) must have felt in summing-up
the case to the jury, as it unquestionably did
something to impair the effect of Clarke's

address. Happily no ill consequences ensued and the prisoner was acquitted; but the danger in a capital case of allowing any interference with the strict order of procedure received a forcible illustration.

It is not often that the suspicion of murder by poison darkens the personal and domestic history of the barrister himself. The tragedy of Charles Bravo's death, however, will never be forgotten by his contemporaries, though all those concerned in the story have long since passed away. He had only been called a year or two, and had sufficient means to live comfortably at Balham without much anxiety about briefs. On one ill-omened morning his friends in the Temple heard that he had died suddenly, after only a few hours' illness. An inquest was held on the body, at which the jury returned an open verdict; but his relations were not satisfied and obtained an order from the Home Secretary for exhumation. The evidence at the second inquiry showed that the dead man had been taken ill an hour or two after a light dinner, and analysis proved that he had been poisoned by a considerable dose of antimony. His wife and a lady who acted as her companion had eaten part of the same dishes, but he himself had taken in addition a couple of glasses of Burgundy, in which it was suggested that the poison was administered. The suspicions of his friends were directed against his wife, who was alleged to have become infatuated with another and a much older man. During his illness Mr. Bravo stated to a medical man that he had taken some laudanum for neuralgia; but it was clear that laudanum had nothing to do with his death, and he assured the doctor that he had taken nothing else. On the other hand, the lady's companion gave evidence that he had told her he had committed suicide. The jury returned a verdict that he had died from the administration of poison by some person unknown, and no further proceedings were instituted. Both the widow and her companion died many years ago, and the "Balham mystery" remains unsolved still.

The defence of insanity, where the facts are beyond dispute, is usually the last resource to which the bewildered advocate turns his mind. It should be—but it is not—the easiest to establish. Mark Twain introduces a metaphysical discussion of Christian science with the preamble " Let us assume that we are all partially insane." So we are—there can be no doubt about it ; though not from the same point of view—as the American philosopher goes on to explain. At any rate, if not permanently insane, we are all subject to " brainstorms." It is perhaps fortunate that physicians and lawyers do not always measure sanity by the same standard. At the trial in 1882 of the notorious Guiteau (the assassin of President Garfield) one expert gave it as his opinion that a large percentage of mankind were " abnormal " so far as their mental condition went. He put it as high as one in five. " That seems rather a large estimate, doesn't it ? " asked the President of the court. " Might take you in, judge ! " ejaculated the criminal, with a self-approving chuckle. The region of sanity we think we know ; and the region of insanity, though beyond our knowledge, we sometimes recognize ; but there is in truth a large borderland, where thousands of us walk unsuspected—and unsuspecting. No criminal lawyer of any experience, for example, will deny the existence of what may be called " blood-lust." I do not mean homicidal mania, or the sudden impulse to kill which so many unhappy creatures avow to the doctor or the chaplain. I am speaking rather of the deliberate and calculated gratification of an unholy passion for the shedding of blood, or for the infliction of painful and agonizing death. One of the most appalling figures in the criminal history of modern years was the murderer Neil Cream. The devilish sport which brought him to the gallows was that of scraping acquaintance with unfortunate women, and administering to them under some pretext or another a deadly and torturing poison. He did not see his victims die; and he must have enjoyed—or at any rate expected to enjoy—the silent gratification of picturing their last agonies to his own foul mind. If demoniac possession still lingers in the Western world, as it is believed by many to do in the East, all the devils of Gadara must have been there as spectators. This, of course, was a very exceptional instance. More common is the simple lust to shed blood—preferably, of a woman—more frequently still, of a child. Of this strange perversion of desire, apparently quite detached from any of the ordinary incidents of human vice, the judges of assize are constantly witnessing examples.   Tested by the ordinary rules, either of jurisprudence or medical science, these men or monsters are not mad.   They are not the victims of illusions or of hallucinations.   They know the difference between right and wrong.   They understand that they will be punished by man if they are detected ; very possibly they believe that they will also be punished by God.   They are simply unable to resist the gratification—or the expected gratification—of the monstrous passion which consumes them.   Other examples—perhaps kindred examples—of perverted sense will readily occur to the criminal expert.   All men —who are not physicians, or lawyers, or theologians—agree in calling this mental state insanity.   But when we pass judgment upon those who walk in the borderland of which I spoke we are less unanimous ; and I do not think that the writings of experts, or even the verbiage of the House of Lords in Macnaghten's case, have given us much assistance.

Juries find less difficulty than judges do in dealing with these abnormal mental conditions.   The despondency, for example, which proceeds from misfortune, poverty, or physical suffering can scarcely be regarded as legal insanity by the jurist, but it is constantly so treated by jurymen, and not only in cases of suicide. Clifton Suspension Bridge has an evil reputation in this regard, and one tragedy which occurred there some five-and-twenty years ago made a deep impression at the time. A small tradesman from Birmingham, distracted by debt and domestic trouble, came to Bristol one gloomy November day with his two children — girls respectively eleven and seven years old. After wandering about aimlessly for some hours, he took them up to Clifton Bridge after dark, and managed to throw them over into the river, nearly three hundred feet below. It was blowing and raining at the time, and the odds against any chance of help must have been incalculable ; but it so happened that there was a boat there rowed by two men on their way home. The children fell one after the other, so close to the boat that one of the rowers had only to stretch out his hand and draw them in. Marvellous to relate, both were alive, and apparently uninjured. Their clothes must, to some extent, have "parachuted," and so diminished the shock of the fall. It is scarcely credible that a boy dressed in trousers could have escaped. The man was tried for attempted murder, but was, of course, found insane and sent to Broadmoor. I was grieved to hear more than a year afterwards that the elder of the two children showed some signs of injury to the spine, but the other was none the worse for her extraordinary experience. The photographs of the two children were exhibited in some of the Bristol shops for a considerable time afterwards. Theirs is not the only instance of a human being surviving the fall from that dreadful height. Some years previously a servant-girl, after a quarrel with her sweetheart, attempted to commit suicide in the same place. The tide was out, and she landed in a half-fluid mixture of mud and water, from which she was rescued, none the worse—after a bath. Her petticoats must have buoyed her up in the same way. It was stated that her boots came off in the fall, which is known to be a common phenomenon in Alpine accidents. I doubt the truth of this part of the story, as it is always supposed that, when this happens, the effect is produced by the air being driven into the boot while the victim is falling head downwards. Boots or no boots, the girl received several offers of marriage immediately after she attained this celebrity, and I trust lived happy ever afterwards. I suppose the inevitable photograph in the newspapers brought about this happy result, and some Jack recognized his predestined and tumbling Jill. Great precautions have been taken of late years to prevent the possibility of suicide from this bridge; but it is almost impossible to protect the rocks at the side, and more than one instance of determined and successful attempt has occurred quite recently. I saw the place first when I was under six years old. The bridge was not then built, and I remember being shown a wire rope stretched across the gorge, with a travelling cage which could carry a man. On one occasion, when Brunel, the engineer, was crossing in this way, the travelling apparatus in some way got fixed, and he remained suspended in the middle for some two hours before he was released. It is difficult to imagine a worse experience of its kind, and I never pass his statue on the Embankment without remembering it.

It is somewhat of a pity that most of the trials for assaults on women are unreportable—there is no class of case in which so many defences of an almost incredible nature succeed. Some, of course, are due to the ingenuity of counsel, but the most extraordinary are often quite genuine. One in particular I remember at Winchester, where the offence had been committed by a cyclist in the daylight of a summer evening. The accused man was seen riding away by two persons in a dog-cart, who kept him in sight for some distance, but were not near enough to see his features. They lost sight of him as he topped the brow of a hill, and when they too reached the summit they still saw what they believed to be the same man on a bicycle two or three hundred yards ahead of them. This man they followed into the town hard by, and he was charged with the offence. But there was a four-cross road just below the brow of the hill, and it was proved satisfactorily enough that the real offender had turned to the left during the few seconds he was out of their sight, while another bicyclist (the man charged) had at the same time entered the main road from the right. They had, in fact, changed their fox ; but it would have gone hard with the prisoner had there not been independent witnesses to prove the route he had really taken. As it was, the jury nearly disagreed.

Cyclists seem liable to trouble of this kind. I remember another case where a cyclist who had ridden from London to Torquay was arrested at the latter place for a like offence committed near Marlborough. Sir Edward Clarke came down to defend him, and succeeded in persuading the jury that the police had got hold of the wrong man. Very likely they had—it sometimes happens. There was once a man put into the dock on a serious charge of this description, who answered to the not uncommon name of John Smith, as did another man in the calendar. When called upon to plead to the indictment, he earnestly protested that a mistake had been made. He was told that he would have an opportunity of addressing the jury later on, and in the meantime he must only say "Not guilty"— which he did. After he had made several futile attempts to interrupt counsel in the narration of his supposed iniquities, the prosecutrix was put into the witness-box and asked to identify him, which she somewhat indignantly refused to do. Persuasion and encouragement proved unavailing, and the judge was ultimately compelled to direct a verdict of acquittal. " All I wanted to say, my lord," observed the prisoner meekly before leaving the dock, "was that what I am really charged with is stealing an umbrella!"

The idiosyncrasy of the judge is a most important factor in trials of this class. Sir John Day had a reputation for severity in all cases involving immorality, and the sentences pronounced by him on the offenders were sometimes terrific. It was said that in many instances he was in the habit of using his influence with the Home Secretary to get them reduced afterwards; and I think it extremely probable, as a kinder-hearted man in reality never lived. Anything indiscreet in the defence, however, always put his back up; and I recollect vividly his indignation in one case where it was pleaded that the prisoner's self-control had been impaired by the habitual use of a drink called "zoedone" —now almost as obsolete as mead or hippocras. Judges naturally dislike trying these cases; and certainly the very plain language necessarily employed by the witnesses must come with something of a shock upon ears more attuned to the Commercial Court. One judge, I remember, whose hearing was somewhat impaired, had acquired the habit of repeating anything that he heard more distinctly than usual, often adding an involuntary expression of satisfaction. The result was sometimes a little embarrassing. "The prisoner called me an a-b-c-d, etc., my lord," said an old woman once at Dorchester. "An a-b-c-d—*good!*" said the judge with gusto, repeating the exact words as he wrote them down with every appearance of gratification. I am afraid some of the junior Bar laughed, but fortunately he did not hear that.

Laughter in court is happily of rare occurrence, except at the witticisms of the Bench. I remember Mr. Justice Denman being much provoked by some manifestation of unseemly mirth at Bodmin. There was an old man there, well known to habitués of the place, whose face was permanently distorted into a ghastly grin. He was in fact a Cornish reproduction of Victor Hugo's "L'homme qui rit." Looking round for the offender, the judge saw this grotesque countenance leaning over the gallery. "You wicked old man," he said in stentorian tones; "I'll send you to prison!" The muscles of the supposed offender's face

remained immovable; and the spectacle of
this hideous grinning countenance looking
down upon the indignant judge upset the
whole court. He was eventually removed
by two policemen, apparently laughing still,
but he evidently felt that he had been treated
with injustice. I have seen him often since
in the streets of Bodmin (still laughing); but
he has been persuaded to discontinue his
attendance at the Assize Court.

The Hon. George Denman, who was the
judge mentioned above, was a man of great
personal dignity and presence. He had been
senior classic at Cambridge, and retained a
love of scholarship throughout his judicial
career. I have a recollection of hearing him
either sing or recite, at some circuit festi-
vity, a Latin version of a ballad about
H.M.S. *Thunderbomb;* and he is said to be
the only judge who attempted to reply in the
same language to a Latin petition, relating to
a half-holiday, which was wont to be addressed
to the senior assize judge by the Winchester
School boys. The objectionable cases at assizes
are very commonly taken together after the
others, and a special day fixed. I once heard
Denman making this announcement at one

of the larger assize towns, when the court was crowded with spectators, including many ladies. " It may be for the convenience of the Bar," he said in a dignified voice, " if I state now that I propose to take all cases— er—of a certain class on next Friday." The discreet silence that ensued was broken by a veteran practitioner, entirely briefless, who happened to be the senior man in court. Rising with evident determination to make the judge's intimation intelligible to all men, he said with emphasis, " Your lordship *means* —the indecent cases ! " Having shed this light on the subject, he sank into his seat with the air of one who had deserved well of his country. It was not the same man, but one like him, who got into trouble before Hawkins, J., when examining a little girl on the *voir dire ;* that is, for the purpose of seeing whether she was competent to be sworn. It is not an easy thing to do, but he was doing it badly ; and Hawkins, who strongly disliked incompetence, refused to allow his questions one after the other. " What would your lordship like me to ask her ? " he said at last in despair. " The proper questions, sir," said the judge in his most acid tones. " Why

M

doesn't he ask her if she knows where she's going when she dies?" said the defending counsel *sotto voce*. The suggestion reached the unhappy man's ear, as it was intended to do, and he promptly acted upon it. The case ended by the judge directing the little witness to leave the box and disallowing the costs of the prosecution. But a very similar question (after some preliminary ones) was once put before Mr. Justice Maule under like circumstances, and answered by a youthful sage of six with great confidence. According to a well-worn story, the learned judge is said to have accepted the evidence forthwith, on the ground that she knew a great deal more than he did.

The alteration in the law, enabling prisoners to give evidence on their own behalf, has greatly increased the chance of conviction in cases of this kind where real guilt exists. The man charged is virtually obliged to tell his own story. This is most beneficial to him if he is innocent, but the guilty man cuts a poor figure in the witness-box. Even before they were allowed to make their statements on oath, prisoners were constantly giving themselves away from the dock. The well-known case of Mrs. Maybrick, who insisted upon speaking after Russell had addressed the jury on her behalf, is an instance in point. She made a most damaging admission, inconsistent with much that her advocate had been urging upon the jury, and it is extremely probable that she would have escaped if she had followed Russell's advice and held her tongue. In cases of minor importance there is often an element of comedy in the situation. A man was being tried at the sessions for the offence of duck-stealing. His counsel addressed the jury for three-quarters of an hour, urging: (1) that the prosecutor had never lost any ducks; (2) that the ducks found in the prisoner's cottage were not the prosecutor's ducks; (3) that the prisoner had established an *alibi* of the clearest possible character. Just as the chairman began to sum up, the prisoner asked if he might say something, and, as an indulgence, he was permitted to have his way. " All I want to say, gentlemen, is just this: I wish I'd never seen the b—— ducks."

One more instance is from the Midland Circuit, and has been told in print before; but the temptation to reproduce it is too strong for me. It was a murder trial, and the real question left in doubt was the identity of the criminal. A common round hat had been found at the scene of the crime, and was said to have been worn by the prisoner. His counsel addressed the jury at great length upon the insufficiency of this evidence, and the hat was produced to them for their inspection. "An ordinary black bowler hat, gentlemen, such as most men wear—such as many of us wear ourselves! It is upon evidence of this flimsy description that you, gentlemen, are invited to pronounce the doom of a fellow-creature—to send to the scaffold," and so on, and so on. The jury were much impressed, and returned a verdict of Not Guilty, and the prisoner was discharged. But he lingered awkwardly in the dock and cast wistful glances around the court, as if something were still weighing upon his heart. The warder tapped him on the shoulder and intimated that another gentleman was waiting to take his place. Then at last he spoke, in a voice husky with emotion. "Beg pardon, your lordship, but—can I 'ave my 'at?"

Prisoners are not always so polite. I recollect the case of one man, who was tried before the then Recorder of Poole—now Sir Arthur Collins. He was a professional acrobat of great physical strength, who earned part of his living by submitting to be bound with ropes in the street and then bursting his bonds like Samson. For some alleged larceny he was committed to the sessions, and in the meantime he was confined in the local prison at Poole. There was only one elderly man in this establishment to discharge the duties of warder, who was completely terrorized by his formidable guest, and the prisoner eventually came up for trial with two indictments against him for assaulting the gaoler, in addition to the original charge. His main defence was that he had not been properly fed ; and he caused to be produced to the court nearly a score of specimens of Irish stew, preserved in large glass jars for the occasion. These he invited the Recorder and myself (as prosecuting counsel) to smell. Collins treated him with the utmost politeness until the jury had convicted him, when he astonished the ruffian by sentencing him to penal servitude for seven years. The prisoner promptly threw a heavy leaden inkstand, which just missed the Recorder's head, and he was then dragged out of the dock by six policemen, declaring in the most frightful language that he would cut out the judicial liver as soon as he was released. Arthur Collins remained on the circuit for six years more, and then applied for and obtained an Indian judgeship—no doubt for the better preservation of the organ indicated. So various are the roads which lead to the judicial Bench.

On the other hand, a little politeness towards offenders is sometimes a useful precaution. A youthful revising barrister, who has since attained very high judicial rank, was once touring in Wales. It is the duty of the civil authorities to detail a policeman for attendance at the Revision Court for the maintenance of order and decorum, and the revising barrister in question had occasion to direct this arm of the law to remove from the court a fisherman who had obviously been drinking. At the end of the day the court adjourned, and the barrister intimated that he would return at the end of a week to complete the business left unfinished. The appointed day arrived, and the barrister was sitting at breakfast in his hotel, when the waiter announced that a visitor wished to see him. The village policeman was ushered in, saluted, and spoke as follows : " Begging your lordship's pardon, but I wish to know what is to be done with the prisoner ! " Visions of an action for false imprisonment, if not of professional ruin, floated before the barrister's eyes ; but he kept his head, and directed that the victim should be brought before him in private. Having harangued him at some length on the enormity of his offence, he presented him with two sovereigns, and told him to go away and lead a better life. Had the culprit refused, the judicial history of this country might have taken a different course.

It seems not unfitting to close this chapter with an admonition which has sometimes recurred to my mind, as I sat idle in a Criminal Court. I cannot give the name of the author, which I have forgotten, if I ever knew it. I can only somewhat narrow the field of inquiry by saying that he was a greater writer than the Circuit Tramp. " Let every one of us endeavour to make an honest man of himself ; and then he may be certain that the world will hold one rascal the less."

CHAPTER VI

TO compare the advocates of the last generation with their successors of the present day would be not only an ungracious task, but a foolish one. To use a sporting metaphor, they have run over different distances with constantly varying weights; and the taste of the public in advocacy is as little permanent as it is in literature. I overheard once at lunch a time-worn Boanerges of the junior Bar confiding his sorrows to the ears of a kindred spirit, his lifelong opponent. " George, my boy," he said plaintively, " our day is over. Go into the Commercial Court, or into Appeal No. 1, and hear Smithson and Heavifee whispering to 'em!" George nodded in silent sympathy, and they sought elsewhere for consolation, which was fortunately at hand. Those who have time for meditation may still, however, find it interesting to recall some of the giants of the past. Speaking of my own circuit first, I never heard Karslake, or "Handsome Jack," as he was sometimes called by his contemporaries. I only saw him once, when illness and physical infirmity had wrecked that once commanding intellect and noble presence— a sorrowful sight. Of Coleridge, his sometime rival, I have already spoken. Certainly I have never heard a voice to compare with his for sheer beauty; and to those who would know something of his great powers I would recommend a perusal of the still celebrated trial of *Saurin v. Starr*, the great convent case, a full report of which is to be found in the libraries of the Inns of Court. His cross-examination of the defendant, the Mother Superior of the convent, was a marvel of tact, delicacy, and effectiveness. Indeed, if I may draw one of the ungracious comparisons which I deprecated a few lines back, I doubt if the cross-examination of the present day is ever quite as impressive or successful as that of the last generation. Hawkins, Ballantine, and Coleridge were masters in this particular branch of advocacy who certainly have not as yet been surpassed —not even by Russell; of whom it was truly said by Charles Bowen that he was an " elemental force."

To express with diffidence my own view, I would say that, while Russell was a great orator, a great cross-examiner, and a great lawyer, he was not in these respects superior to all others—not even to all his contemporaries. But as a great personality and an " elemental force," Russell was more than pre-eminent—he was overwhelming.

Huddleston was another very successful advocate in an entirely different class. He had the great merit of always being on excellent terms with his jury, and retained the same happy knack after his elevation to the Bench. Many of us nowadays are afraid of them, which is almost a worse error than being afraid of the judge. Nine-tenths of what the newspapers call " scenes in court" —which is a euphemism for collisions between the Bench and the Bar—are really due to this latter failing. It is commoner than it appears to outsiders, and even, I think, than it need be. Probably a judge never inspires more awe than when sitting in chambers, but even there they have been known to unbend. A particularly timid junior was once told that his summons must be adjourned to the following Friday. "I hope your lordship will not say Friday," said the barrister in a supplicatory tone. "But I *shall* say Friday," answered the judge, "unless you have a good reason to the contrary. What engagement have you for that day?" The barrister explained, with diffidence, that the christening of his first-born child was appointed for that date. "Not another word!" said his lordship benevolently. "Say Friday week — Friday fortnight—any day you like, Mr. A." The proud parent was effusive in his thanks, but just as he reached the door a happy thought struck him, and he returned to the table. "As your lordship has been so kind," he whispered modestly, "perhaps your lordship would consent to be godfather!" Nothing would give his lordship greater pleasure, and godfather he was. A touch of domesticity went even further in the case of another junior, whom we will call B. He had been supporting a summons at chambers for leave to administer interrogatories; and Mr. Justice Denman, after going carefully through the draft, had struck out a considerable part of it, yielding to the strenuous objections of a little solicitor's clerk on the other side. B. was personally known to the judge, who was aware that he had just returned from his honeymoon. So his lordship, after having disposed of the interrogatories, said kindly, " Now, Mr. B., you must permit me to congratulate you." " I don't think your lordship need do that," interposed the solicitor's clerk jealously. " He hasn't got half as much as he expected ! "

The most humorous advocate I remember at the Bar was certainly Sir John Day, renowned (amongst other things) for his taciturnity during the Parnell inquiry. It may seem disrespectful to mention that his features lent themselves to facial display, but it is an historical fact that those who were too far off to hear what he said laughed almost as much as listeners who were better placed. But he never forgot the jury, and was a great verdict-getter, as well as a really good lawyer, which does not always follow. He managed, however, to conceal his humour by writing a book on the Common Law Procedure Acts— no doubt as a much-needed relief from jesting.

For a contrast to the style of Day one turns naturally to Lincoln's Inn. Of the many great lawyers but monotonous speakers who have achieved fame and fortune in the Chancery Courts, Sir Horace Davey—afterwards a Lord Justice and a Lord of Appeal—may be selected as a typical example. The intellectual effort necessary to follow his utterances was always considerable; and the absence of anything like animation in his voice and delivery was so ostentatious, that one sometimes wondered how he had forced himself into prominence at all. One may assume that even at the Common Law Bar his great ability would have asserted itself, but no one could be surprised that his electioneering experiences were not brilliantly successful. He could afford, however, to smile at the oratorical arts which others found indispensable; and few advocates can have made more money in so short a time. When he was made a Lord Justice of Appeal his clerk must have been one of the most disappointed men in England. "Well, I did think" —he is reported to have said—"I *did* think that Sir 'Orris had a couple more years' work left in him!"

It would be impossible to omit the name of Hardinge Giffard from this brief review, which must therefore have remained unwritten if

Lord Halsbury still occupied the Woolsack. The most strenuous and resolute of fighters, in the courts as in the House of Commons, he was equally remarkable for versatility; and he seemed to "specialize" in every branch of advocacy, as in turn he took up each. He led for the defendant in the first civil cause in which I ever held a brief, my seniors being Prideaux, Q.C., and Arthur Charles. Hardinge Giffard and W. Willis (the present County Court judge) were the counsel opposed to us; and they pulled the case out of the fire on appeal after we had won before Kelly, C.B., and a special jury. I need hardly say that my own efforts were wisely restricted by my leaders to note-taking. Giffard was always marvellous in reply, and made more use than any one I have heard of the advantage of the "last word." I remember one example, where he appeared for the plaintiff in an action for slander, against some members of a charitable association. The defendants' counsel had quoted the passage from the New Testament which defines true religion as being "to visit the widows and the fatherless in their affliction, and to keep oneself unspotted from the world." "My friend has forgotten the text which follows," said Giffard. "'If any man amongst you seemeth to be religious, *and bridleth not his own tongue*, that man's religion is vain.'" Nobody in court knew whether this followed the quotation or not, but in fact it immediately precedes it.

Of those who practised more especially in the Criminal Courts, in addition to some of the men I have already named, Montagu Williams was perhaps the most conspicuous and successful. Admirable of its kind, I do not think his somewhat theatrical and artificial style would at the present day escape some criticism; but as a defender of prisoners he had at one time few equals. One of the last important trials in which I heard him was known at the time as the "Detective case."

Three well-known members of the detective staff at Scotland Yard, together with a solicitor, were being tried at the Old Bailey in 1877 for complicity in the frauds of two notorious criminals named Kurr and Benson. The last-mentioned couple had already been convicted and sentenced for defrauding an old French lady named de Goncourt, and they had been brought up from prison to give evidence against the detectives. Montagu

Williams defended one of the prisoners, and the vigour of his phraseology gave a new idea of criminal advocacy to one at least of his audience. "Excellent in vice and exquisite in fraud—the cunning of a cat teeming from the eyes of one; the oily soft serpent-like treachery of deceit trickling from the mouth of the other"—the souls of Dangerfield and Titus Oates seemed to the speaker to have passed into their bodies! Few indeed are the advocates nowadays who could venture upon such flights without exciting derision; but the best proof of his real power was that no one laughed at Montagu Williams. More than thirty years have passed since I witnessed that scene, and I still have a vivid mental picture of his virile and dramatic figure, attacking the Treasury counsel almost as vigorously as the witnesses, and winding up an impassioned invective against something that sounded like subornation of perjury, by denouncing to a gaping jury what he picturesquely called "the tactics of the opposition"! In this special instance his client did not escape; but the innumerable miscarriages of justice produced by his oratory were ample compensation for an occasional reverse. The last time I heard him was at the trial of the notorious poisoner Lamson, at the Old Bailey in 1882 ; and I remember that in his speech to the jury, Montagu Williams declared that he felt the responsibility of his position to be such that he would never willingly incur it again. In fact, I believe it was the last occasion on which he defended a man charged with the capital offence. His health began to fail soon afterwards, and he was appointed a London police-magistrate, in which capacity, during the short remnant of his life, he did admirable public service.

Sir John Holker, Henry James (Lord James of Hereford), and Henry Matthews (Lord Llandaff) were three other conspicuous advocates of the last generation. Holker was massive and deliberate, with a hesitating delivery that amounted at times almost to a stammer, but he could address a jury as if he was one of themselves, and won their confidence by his apparent sincerity rather than by a parade of oratorical power. He became Solicitor-General under Mr. Disraeli's Government in 1874, and succeeded Sir Richard Baggallay as Senior Law Officer in

N

the following year. The Conservative tenure of power was short-lived; and the vacancies caused by the deaths of Sir Alexander Cockburn and Sir Fitzroy Kelly did not occur until after the fall of the Government; but the Liberal Government paid Holker the exceptional compliment of appointing him a Lord Justice of Appeal in succession to Lord Justice Lush—probably the only case in which an ex-law-officer of one political party was promoted by the other. Henry James and Henry Matthews were both stars of the Oxford Circuit, which has certainly enjoyed its full share of distinction during the present generation, and still boasts not only of the Lord Chancellor himself, but of three other judges (Darling, Jelf, and Lawrence, JJ.), in addition to those I have named. The custom of wearing a powdered wig was cherished on this circuit long after it had been abandoned elsewhere. Huddleston, Henry James, and Matthews were all wont to appear with this effective but troublesome adjunct to forensic dignity, and I think I remember that Mr. Justice Darling once followed their example. I doubt not that the archives of the Oxford Circuit contain some explanation of this peculiarity, and it is perhaps to be regretted that so picturesque an adornment has fallen into disuse.

The most conspicuous figures on the Common Law Bench when my recollections begin were Cockburn, C.J., and Chief Baron Kelly. Cockburn was a little man, with a wonderfully resonant voice and much judicial dignity. He was still remembered in the West of England as a member of the circuit, and I met at least half a dozen ancient solicitors who boasted of having given him his first brief; but looking at him on the Bench, it was difficult to believe that the stories of his tempestuous youth at sessions had any foundation in fact. The well-known caricature of him by Frank Lockwood gave a better idea of his expressive and dominating features than any other likeness I have seen. Fitzroy Kelly seemed to belong to a more antiquated school —a type of precision, courtesy, and refinement. I was told that when Attorney-General, in the year of the first great Exhibition in Hyde Park, he received over fifty thousand pounds in patent fees alone—a source of emolument which it is to be feared no longer enriches the law officers of the Crown. In his old age

he was a little fidgety and impatient of in-
accuracies. " Will you be good enough to
give me the dates ? " was a favourite request
of his. " I have already given your lordship
the material dates," counsel once answered
somewhat rashly. "Then be good enough
now to give me the immaterial ones," the
Chief Baron replied, and progress, until he
got them, became impossible. Baron Bramwell was another conspicuous personality on
the Bench. He it was who invented the well-
known classification of perverters of the truth
—" liars, d——d liars, and expert witnesses."
At a later date he added a fourth class—
" my brother Frederick," meaning, of course,
Sir Frederick Bramwell, perhaps the best-
known expert engineer witness of his day,
who survived the judge many years. Bramwell ultimately became a Lord of Appeal,
and in that capacity did not always agree
with the judgments delivered by his col-
leagues. It may be that he occasionally
doubted the correctness of some of his own.
" There ought to be a Statute of Limitations
to protect judges against their old *obiter
dicta*," I heard him say once in the Court of
Appeal. At the Bar his language was some-

times a little unconventional. " Are you sure of that, Mr. Bramwell ? " he was once asked by a learned judge after a somewhat unexpected statement of fact. " Cock ! my lord ! " was Bramwell's vigorous reply, which completely satisfied the Bench. I do not know any barrister of recent days, except perhaps Sir Charles Russell, who was able to address the judges in language quite so unceremonious. He was not readily put off his line of argument, even by the Court of Appeal, which in his day gave the advocate little rope. Russell had an off-hand way of ignoring judicial interruption, which it would not be prudent for every beginner to emulate. "Aye, aye ! but I was about to say something else ! " he observed to that illustrious body once in my hearing. I remember breathing a fervent aspiration that I might myself one day be adventurous enough to say, " Aye, aye ! " to the Court of Appeal.

The Bench, on the other hand, were sometimes a little unconventional in their attitude towards the Bar. There was one judge (long since dead) who was in the habit of coming on the Western Circuit as often as he could. It will be admitted, I am sure, that this

N 2

peculiarity affords little clue to his name. He was trying a cause at Dorchester, conducted by two juniors, in which a jury had been dispensed with by consent. It was an action by a house-agent for commission, and judgment was given for the plaintiff in substantially the following terms: " Mr. Jones says this money was very easily earned. So it is in all professions. For example, you might go to Mr. Jones for an opinion, and he might dash you off something in ten minutes that might not be worth the paper it was written upon." Jones rose furious from his seat, and lifted a leaden inkstand in his hands—I suppose to hurl at his traducer. But the judge waved him down with, " Stay, please! Or you might go to Mr. Brown " (the counsel on the other side), " who might take ten days over it, and it mightn't be worth much more!" Then both learned counsel understood that the judge was pleased to jest, and a wan smile of intelligence stole over their faces.

A still more disconcerting attitude was not unfrequently adopted by another late member of the Bench. He was wont to declare that he never listened to the "opening" of counsel;

and to do him justice, he seldom did. His theory, no doubt, was that a correct apprehension of the case could only be gathered from the evidence, and he preferred accordingly to wait for the witnesses; but the indignity of seeing the judge deliberately reading the newspaper, while a perhaps youthful barrister was opening his case to the jury, was considerable. The only consolation of the advocate was to witness the same learned judge nodding after lunch—which sometimes happened. I remember seeing the shorthand notes of an appeal from a judgment of his— notes which I believe were afterwards read *in extenso* to the House of Lords. The conscientious shorthand writer had taken down and transcribed a *sotto voce* remark made by A. L. Smith, L.J., to Lord Esher, which was certainly never intended for the reporter's ear. "If I had just had a couple of mutton-chops and a bottle of stout for lunch," said the Lord Justice to the President, "I could understand myself delivering this judgment." But the somnolent one was a very able judge, notwithstanding his peculiarities; and his dislike to opening speeches may perhaps be forgiven him. Openings are generally irritating, and often dull. Sir John Rigby, afterwards a Lord Justice of Appeal, once pathetically implored the judge to allow his opponent's somewhat involved speech to run its course. " My friend's opening is already obscure," said Rigby. " With your lordship's interruptions it becomes unintelligible ! " This was, of course, in one of the Chancery Courts, when the relationship between the Bench and the Bar is often of a more confidential nature than on the Common Law side. I can only recall one instance in which this was disturbed by what I once heard an Attorney-General, on the retirement of a judge (now deceased) describe euphemistically as "friction." This was thirty years ago, when the leading advocate in the Court of Vice-Chancellor Malins created a scene by complaining of the dilatoriness in that particular court, and the consequent arrest of business—particularly his own. At that period it seemed almost profane to quarrel with the leisured dignity of Chancery procedure. Times have changed since then, and we are accustomed to the spectacle of Chancery judges who have cleared their own lists, and are brought in to assist their brethren of the King's Bench Di-

vision in the despatch of "non-juries." I doubt
if any legal practitioner would be expert
enough, apart from personal knowledge, to detect the difference between the two. Lest I
should be misunderstood, I hasten to add that
I do not suggest that any difference exists.
Distinction is a better word, and one of which
surely no one can complain. At any rate,
I do not remember any Common Law judge
having an egg thrown at him in court, as
once happened to the Vice-Chancellor of
whom I have just spoken; or even rivalling
the experiences of Sir George Jessel, who
narrowly escaped being shot by a lunatic
named Dodwell when sitting as Master of
the Rolls. I have certainly seen a leaden
inkstand thrown at a recorder; but in the
case of such a minor functionary, this may
almost be regarded as a legitimate form of
criticism.

Judges, however, whether on circuit or elsewhere, are seldom indeed inconsiderate of the
professional interests of the Bar—especially
the junior Bar. I never heard of an assize
judge placing himself in an undignified position, save on one memorable occasion at
Bristol. It was a time when the dynamite

scare was raging, and those members of the Bench who had taken part in the resulting trials were under the protection of detectives. By some extraordinary accident, while the judges and the Bar were being entertained at dinner by the Lord Mayor of Bristol, the lights suddenly failed and the room was thrown into absolute darkness. It was stated—but I do not personally vouch for the truth of the story—that when candles were brought, one of Her Majesty's judges was found emerging from beneath the table, where he had taken refuge from an expected attack by Fenians. Judicial discretion was in this case the better part of valour. Fortunately, it was after he had returned thanks for the toast of his health; and he was able to make a hurried return to the judges' lodgings without scandal.

I have not yet, I think, spoken (either respectfully or otherwise) of any of His Majesty's judges who still occupy seats upon the Bench—that is, in their judicial capacity; and I propose to deny myself that natural gratification. They manage these things differently in the United States. I have been recently solicited by post to purchase a work

by an American lawyer, entitled *Foibles of
the Bench*. Now I will not go so far as to
assert that no members of the English Bench
have ever any foibles; but certainly they are
not of the kind depicted by the ingenious
author I have mentioned. According to this
writer—not an anonymous one—it was a
foible of one American judge (with whom he
says that he was personally acquainted), to
have inherited from his mother dyspepsia,
and from his father biliousness. It was a
foible to have added to his inheritance by his
habits several other diseases which became
chronic. It was a foible to be as lean as
a hyæna, and as yellow as saffron; to have
a voice with a thin nasal twang; to have
a tongue of which no one, down to the bailiff
of the court, could escape the venom; and
to keep the atmosphere about the Bench
"streaked with sulphur." I do not suppose
that these rhetorical flowers are considered
amusing in America, or it would not be
necessary to advertise for readers of them
in England; but the terror of such an example would be enough to deter any English
writer, however presumptuous, from entering
upon the subject of judicial foibles at all.

It will not, however, be deemed disrespectful if I illustrate my own sentiments on the subject by one more anecdote, for which the Western Circuit is responsible. One of our present judges was recently trying a case in which he was urged by the counsel for the defendant to rule that there was no evidence for the jury, and he observed that if he did the Court of Appeal would probably say that he was wrong. " I don't think there is any chance of that, my lord," said the advocate cheerfully. " Well, you probably know the Appeal judges better than I do," answered the learned judge. " You hear them in court—I never see them except at lunch." " Your lordship, no doubt, sees them *at their best*," was the dry reply, delivered in tones of the utmost solemnity and respect.

There is one class of advocates—if advocates they may be called—to which I have not yet referred, but which deserves a passing glance —I mean litigants in person. They are the terror of the Bar, and (with some fortunate exceptions) the aversion of the Bench. One well-known lady litigant owed much of her success to the fact that she excited the admiration of both ; and indeed, between her

and a high judicial dignitary, there sprang up
at one time almost a forensic flirtation. Her
example was unfortunately followed by others
who possessed fewer natural advantages; and
at one time amateur litigation of this class
seemed to have become epidemic. One well-
known figure, with an impossible name, used to
appear every Monday morning in the Court of
Appeal. I do not know if he was a Russian
or a Pole, but he had a grievance against
Lloyd's, which for some years he persistently
attempted to reopen. Nobody in court—I
believe no one in London—could understand
a word he said, except Lord Justice A. L.
Smith, to whom he was accustomed to
address himself in guttural tones which
seemed to inexperienced ears to be scarcely
human. That learned judge was wont to ask
him to put his complaint into writing, which
he had always done in anticipation of such
a request, and he was usually pacified by
a promise that his documents should be read
and considered. I believe his original action
was against the underwriters of a ship, which
he had been accused of having scuttled. I
never heard that there was any ground for
this imputation, except his personal appear-

ance, which suggested a Guy Fawkes of Yiddish origin. There was an old lady who used to haunt the Court of Appeal in the same decade, and always jumped up in the well of the court when *ex párte* motions were being taken. In my own junior days I was for some years opposed to another charming old woman, who was a veritable reincarnation of " Miss Flite," and looked as if she had just stepped out of *Bleak House*, reticule and all. Her name was Jenner, and she had a hopeless claim to some Welsh estates, as well as an imaginary grievance against the National Provincial Bank, which she fought with extraordinary persistence and perfect courtesy. I appeared for the bank, and was constantly receiving quaint little notes from her making appointments to meet at judges' chambers, where she was a well-known figure. She was connected with the family of the late Sir Herbert Jenner Fust, who was (I think) Dean of the Court of Arches, a fact to which she always gave due prominence in her affidavits. Her litigation never did her any good ; but I think she enjoyed it, and it certainly did no one else any harm. If she is ever reincarnated I hope the particulars for which I so often applied in vain will be forthcoming.

There was another litigant in person, bearing a well-known legal name, of whom my recollections are less placid. He was an elderly man, like Ally Sloper when viewed from behind and the " White Knight " when seen in front ; with a perfectly bald, egg-shaped head, and enormous ears which flapped when he got excited. Eventually I escaped from the constant misery of appearing against him by taking refuge in circuit engagements, and he fell into other hands. His grievance was against a solicitor, but I never heard whether he made anything of it in the end, though I believe Cave, J., directed some inquiry to be held into the matter. The task of arguing against such an opponent used to leave in my mind a sense almost of degradation. No doubt I produced the same impression upon him. None of the litigants in person whom I have heard showed any real ability, with the exceptions of Mrs. Weldon, Mr. Bottomley, Mr. Bradlaugh, and Baron Grant. Most of them were really unable to make themselves understood. I think there can be no doubt that a taste for this sort of publicity becomes in time a monomania, arising from the "exaggerated ego" of which medical experts now tell us. Fortunately the cases of it which occur in the Criminal Court are rare, the advantages of having a "mouthpiece" being generally recognized by the professional wrong-doer. If committed to prison before trial, he frequently obtains from a warder the names of the best-known advocates who are likely to be present at his trial, in order to select one on whom to bestow a "dock brief" for his defence. I remember one man at Exeter who called out the names of no less than seven barristers, in strict order of merit, before he hit upon one who was in court. I knew instinctively that my own name was the eighth, and hid myself in the robing-room. As a contrast to this appreciation of the professional assistance of the Bar, one recalls to mind the drawing of Charles Keene in *Punch* some twenty years ago. The prisoner, who is supposed to be on bail, is being introduced by his solicitor to the counsel who has been retained for his defence, with whose stature and personal appearance he is unfavourably impressed. "What! '*im* my counsellor?" says the dissatisfied client. "Blowed if I don't appear in person!"

The excessive tenderness, which has manifested itself of late years towards the prisoner on his trial, has greatly multiplied his opportunities of obtaining professional assistance. Some years ago the members of a certain county sessions Bar were moved by compassion to pass a rule, by which they took it in turns to defend gratuitously those prisoners who were not represented in the ordinary way. This was successfully challenged, I think, by the Bar Council, as a breach of professional etiquette ; but it was the indirect cause of the passing of the Poor Prisoners' Defence Bill, under which any prisoner who is without means may apply to the judge, recorder, or chairman (as the case may be) to have a solicitor and counsel assigned to him at the expense of a sympathetic country. The application is not always granted, as this assistance is theoretically limited to cases in which some defence has been disclosed before the magistrates ; but it is granted oftener than it deserves to be. I remember one instance in my own experience, where a prisoner had unsuccessfully offered through a solicitor a fee of ten guineas for the services of a King's Counsel, and afterwards took the benefit of

o

the Poor Prisoners' Defence Act on the plea
of poverty. If the persecuted victim does
not like to run his chances under this Act,
he may choose his own counsel from those
present in court for the sum of one pound
three and sixpence. These dock defences
are quite frequent at the Central Criminal
Court, and common enough on circuit and at
sessions. Lastly, if his case is at all a serious
one, he may appeal to the judge to ask some
member of the Bar to defend him gratuitously;
and, indeed, I have never known an assize
judge omit to take this course, of his own
accord, in the case of an undefended capital
charge. Great anxiety was shown, when the
Poor Prisoners' Defence Act was passed, that
its benefits should be duly made known to all
prisoners under remand; and it was even
suggested—I think before the Bar Council—
that a list of the counsel willing to accept
defences under it should be hung up in every
cell, together with an abstract of the statute.
I have not the personal experience necessary
to enable me to say if this brilliant scheme
was carried into effect; but I have reason
to believe that in some prisons, at any rate,
either the governor or the chaplain or the chief

warder (or all three) will supply the prisoners awaiting trial with a list of counsel accurately classified in order of merit, to whom dock defences may be delivered. It has been done in the past, at any rate--let us hope that the practice has ceased with the necessity for it. But it is obvious that the average prisoner, in selecting his champion, may easily have an *embarras de richesses;* and that the walls of his cell might be papered with notices that would afford quite interesting reading to the junior Bar. I am not sure that these extended facilities for defence are an un-mixed good. That a larger percentage of defended prisoners are acquitted than of those not so assisted is perfectly true; but I am afraid it does not follow that they deserve it. Every one is familiar with the consequences when *nocens absolvitur;* but for my part, I confess that my sympathy lies rather with the *damnatus judex*, who is more frequent than he ought to be.

CHAPTER VII

ON EVIDENCE

THE art of giving evidence is one of which the Circuit Tramp has no personal experience; but with some of the methods of eliciting —or concealing—it he is not unfamiliar. It has been stated by some who ought to have known better, that the examination of witnesses "in chief" is the most difficult branch of the advocate's art; and the young beginner used at one time to be taught to take a careful note of his leader's opening, and to examine the witness from that rather than from his proof. There are obvious dangers in taking this advice, especially if the leader has not had time to read his brief. It has been said with more apparent reason, that it was to meet this possible contingency, that the practice was introduced of entrusting the first and most important witness to the hands of the junior counsel.

I am not so besotted as to imagine that any words of mine can be read with profit by those upon whom this task usually devolves. I would rather, if I could, assist the witness himself, which indeed is the main function of the examining counsel, though he often appears to the average layman rather to be impeding than aiding the volunteer of Truth. The reason, no doubt, of this is, that the barrister knows far better than the witness what the Truth really is, inasmuch as he has it all written down for him by the solicitor in the form of a "proof," which it is his business to see that the witness reproduces without any conceited display of originality or invention. More actions are, in fact, lost by the foolish neglect by the witnesses of this primary rule, than in any other way. This has been recognized by the wisdom of the Chancery Courts, where it has been long usual for the witness to append his signature to the "proof" out of court, in order that it may be presented bodily to the judge after having been re-christened as an "affidavit." This is the ideal system, to which the joint efforts of witness and counsel should strive as closely as possible to approximate.

The object of the opposing counsel, who sometimes invokes for this purpose the unholy

assistance of the judge, is to prevent this ideal
from being attained, by raising captious objections, and so hindering the examiner from telling the witness what the proof really contains.
It is customary for policemen, who realize the
importance of simple veracity better than
most other persons, to meet this manœuvre
by the useful expedient of learning their proofs
by heart ; but the average witness has neither
the time nor the ability to take this course,
which indeed cannot be recommended for
general adoption. The young advocate, therefore, has to learn how to put leading questions
without being stopped by the judge ; and it is
a common device for this purpose to be ostentatiously careful in avoiding this offence, so
long as nothing can be gained by committing
it. I think, however, that higher art is dis-
played by accustoming the ears of your
opponent, from the beginning, to the style
of interrogation which is likely to prove most
useful in the end. Thus have I heard an Irish
advocate, a master of his craft, commence in
the following way : " Patrick Rooney, h'what's
y'r name ? " " Patrick Rooney, sorr," was the
simple and satisfying response ; and the witness, finding the first question so easy to

answer, looked confidently for like assistance in those which followed : nor was he disappointed.

The nervousness of an inexperienced witness, which adds so much to the difficulties of his examiner, is usually due to a mistaken idea that he is for the time the most important person in court. I need not say that this is an entire fallacy, but the same mistake is made by other characters in the piece. The plaintiff and the defendant both think the same. So do their leading counsel ; so (very often) do the juniors, on the ground that they drew the pleadings and advised on evidence. The judge himself is occasionally not free from a subconsciousness of the same kind. The solicitor for the plaintiff may be forgiven for a like conception of his own merits, when he reflects (as he sometimes can) that but for him the action would never have been brought at all. Long and bitter experience, however, has persuaded me that they are all wrong. The prisoner in a criminal case, the respondent in a divorce suit, the junior counsel in a breach of promise who reads the defendant's letters to the reporters—all in their several positions have a distinction of their own. But taking one case with another, whether in the provinces or in London, and from the beginning of the trial to the end, the coveted pre-eminence must be awarded to one who never opens his lips, and who is unconscious of the justice of his claim. The most important personage in court, to whose level all strive to rise or fall, is without doubt the stupidest member of the jury.

The junior barrister who attempts the arduous task of taking a conscientious witness through his proof will probably experience his first difficulty when he has to induce the victim to repeat the words of some one else. It is a popular error, based on the ruling of Mr. Justice Stareleigh in *Bardell v. Pickwick*, that what the soldier said is never admissible as evidence. To enumerate the exceptions to this perfectly sound rule would be a tedious and unprofitable task. Suffice it to say that they are not infrequent, and that it is comparatively rare to meet a witness who can repeat the remarks of a third person with the accuracy of the immortal Sam Weller. The prudent man usually qualifies his testimony by the superfluous statement that he cannot remember the exact words, but is willing to tell the court what he understood the speaker to mean. " The prisoner's wife stood at the bottom of the stairs and called out, ' Tom, Tom,' *or words to that effect*," is a classical illustration of this kind of imperfect recollection. In the action of *Clarke v. Bradlaugh*, brought against the famous member for Northampton to recover penalties for having voted in Parliament without taking the oath, the Serjeant-at-Arms of the House of Commons was called to prove what actually took place when Mr. Bradlaugh attempted to administer the oath to himself. Being a very conscientious man, and alive to the importance of the occasion, he prefaced his evidence by observing that he would not attempt to repeat the precise words used by the Speaker. He gave a fairly graphic description, however, of Mr. Bradlaugh's attempt to storm the sanctuary, and made it evident that something very like an altercation had ensued, with some warmth on both sides. " And then it was," he proceeded, " that the Speaker made use of words which I cannot—which I will not repeat." It is to be hoped that there are no grounds for suggesting that Mr. Peel's language on this occasion was unreportable, but some ribald laughter was heard in court at this account of it. Yet this witness, after all, understood the difference between *oratio recta* and *oratio obliqua*, which it is absolutely impossible to convey to the uneducated. Judge and counsel are equally helpless before a witness who is determined to repeat what he has heard in the third person. He may, for example, be anxious to explain that a prisoner charged with duck-stealing has confessed his guilt. " He said he stole the duck " is probably the form of language he will select for this purpose. It is useless to tell him to repeat the exact words, or not to speak in the third person, or to imagine himself the person speaking. He will only reply that those *are* the exact words, that he is speaking the truth, and that there was no third person there. " He could not have said 'he stole the duck,'" a learned judge is said to have once interposed. "What you mean is that he said 'I stole the duck.'" "He never mentioned your lordship's name," was the earnest and apologetic reply ; and the court had to be contented with *oratio obliqua* after all. Witnesses of a certain class, when they do stray into the first person by accident, are wont to emphasize the fact in a way of their own. One of the London police-magistrates was recently taking the night charges, when a lady whose conduct was complained of asked for an interpreter. " She don't want no interpreter," scornfully observed the policeman in the witness-box. " But she says she can't speak English," said the magistrate. " She spoke very good English about one a.m. this morning," replied the officer. " What did she say ? " inquired the magistrate curiously. " Well, sir," answered the witness, " I said ' Move on,' says I, just like that, and then she says 'This is a free country, I suppose,' says she, 'and you're only a blooming copper,' she says. ' And as for the beak,' says she, ' he —— ' " But here the magistrate observed that an interpreter would not be necessary and that the defendant evidently spoke very good English indeed.

Legal objections, however, to questions which are leading, or which invite the repetition of hearsay, are only made to be overcome. It is usual for the judge, when compelled to exclude an inquiry of this character, to ask the examining counsel to " put it in another form." The substituted form is generally equally irregular, but has a better chance of passing The judge's suggestion implies that there is some form in which the question may be put ; but it is very often the case that neither he nor the advocate knows what that form is. This is the examiner's opportunity to produce a general impression that he understands the judicial suggestion better than its author. This little artifice is invaluable, but it wants experience to give it plausibility. In raw hands it only invites rebuke. During the progress of the second Dreyfus trial, I heard a judge in one of our own courts assign a novel reason for rejecting an interrogatory of this character at the second attempt. " I shall not allow that question," his lordship said firmly. " An exactly similar one was put yesterday, without objection, at Rennes." This was an application of private international law which proved too much for the offender, and he gave up the struggle. The art of putting inadmissible questions is one in which solicitors in the County Courts are often adepts. I once heard an advocate of this class endeavouring to prove his client's version of the contract between him and the defendant. " Your agreement with the defendant was, I believe," he began, and then proceeded to read it from the proof. "Put it in the form of a question," said the judge benevolently. " Did you tell me that——" " No, no," said the judge, a little less benevolently. " Am I under the impression that you told me that you agreed ——" At this stage the judge took the witness out of the advocate's hands, and the plaintiff proceeded to correct the impression he had made upon his solicitor by proving the case for the defendant without delay. The ingenuity of that advocate was wasted in the County Courts. He should have gone to the Parliamentary Bar, where there is a tacit understanding that objections to leading questions are not in good taste. I once, however, heard a chairman of a Lords Committee himself essay the task of keeping a well-known offender in order, and pull him up again and again for violation of elementary rules. The eminent counsel in question bore it patiently for some time, but at last the unwonted restraint proved too much for him. Folding up his papers ostentatiously, he turned to his junior before leaving the room, and remarked in a perfectly audible voice, " I think it's about time to change the bowling ! " So, in cricket phraseology, he " took himself off."

Of re-examination, as it is most commonly

understood and practised, it is almost sufficient to say that too many advocates regard it
as an opportunity for calling upon the witness
to repeat his story over again, as if he had
been encored. Its more legitimate uses are
to restore the witness to the pedestal of re-
spectability from which he has been rudely
deposed ; and occasionally to introduce new
facts which were either immaterial or inadmissible before the cross-examination. This
was the old-fashioned idea ; but now that
cases are tried without pleadings, or with
pleadings which are amended if read, all the
immaterial facts can usually be elicited without difficulty in the course of the examination-in-chief ; and counsel often finds the privilege of re-examining most useful for asking
those questions which he has forgotten to put
in their proper place. I have indeed seen
witnesses recalled for this purpose, not only
after the case has been closed, but even after
the judge had finished his summing-up—or
thought he had. It is therefore better to
be pertinacious than to be correct ; and every
leader should remember that a *locus pœni-
tentiæ* is more likely to be granted to his
junior, if he himself is called upon to leave

the court. For the purpose of rehabilitating a witness whose plumage has been ruffled, the example of a well-known Chancery leader, in the early days of the Judicature Act, may be borne in mind with advantage. " You have been asked by my learned friend," said the advocate suavely, " whether you have not on a previous occasion been tried on a criminal charge and convicted. I ask you if it is not also true that on three other occasions, of which you can give the dates if required, you were put on your trial for a similar offence and *acquitted!*" Except for this benign purpose of whitewashing the besmirched, it may be doubted whether re-examination proper is worth the time bestowed upon it. It is much easier to interrupt a cross-examiner when he seems to threaten mischief, than to attempt to remove the effect after it has been produced. And though judges often declare that they are loth to interfere with cross-examination so long as it is not obviously being abused, there is no reason why counsel on the other side should be so squeamish. On the other hand, it should be borne in mind that the best witness is he who re-examines himself; and those eminent persons who are called to give expert evidence in rating and compensation cases are probably the best exponents of this art. So long as they do not insist upon going a step further, and making the speeches which they think should have been made by their counsel, there is no great harm in indulging their desire. The expert witness is so often suspected of placing science before veracity, that he may usefully be permitted a chance of showing how the two may be reconciled, however seldom that may be possible.

Lastly, there is found a very general consensus of opinion that the rule against putting leading questions does not apply to re-examination. Were it not for this beneficent exception to the ordinary principles of law, it would indeed be difficult for the average advocate to re-examine at all. The task of suggesting to a truthful witness that it is desirable either to contradict or explain away an answer which he has already given is never an easy one; and when the proper explanation is known to the advocate but not to the witness, it is obvious that unless he is allowed to put a leading question the re-examiner may as well sit down. The dignity of the Bar does not allow such a confession of impotence, and the leading question is invariably put. If an objection is taken by a too punctilious opponent, it is a sufficient excuse to assert that the witness "has said it already." The pedant may perhaps complain that this justification of a common practice is inadequate, but it must be remembered that " *quod semper, quod ubique, quod ab omnibus*" has in all ages obtained the blind acceptance of the faithful.

The one person who may, without danger of rebuke, put words into the witness's mouth, is, of course, the judge himself. It is sometimes done with incongruous results. The master of a vessel which had run aground was once giving evidence, and stated that he was well aware at the time that the pilot was taking a wrong course. Being asked by the judge why he had not told the pilot so at the critical moment, he replied, " What could I have said to the pilot?" " Well," said the judge suavely, "you might have said, ' You goose! don't you see you are endangering the safety of the ship?'" But this excellent imitation of nautical phraseology did not commend itself to the witness. A judge, indeed, often strays into humour without knowing it.

P

I remember an election petition in which one allegation was, that a number of rosettes, or "marks of distinction," had been kept in a table-drawer in the central committee-room. To meet this charge, it was thought desirable to call witnesses to swear that the only table in the room consisted of planks laid upon trestles. "So that the table had no proper legs?" said counsel cheerfully. "Never mind whether it had proper legs," said one of the learned judges. "The more important question is, had it drawers?"

CROSS-EXAMINATION

To state the bald, pitiable truth, that cross-examination has become a lost art, will not, I hope, give offence to any of its numerous living professors. Every one must recognize that this is not from any lack of ability in the advocates of the present day, and I think the only real explanation of the disappearance of this accomplishment is that its exercise—like that of oratory—has become unfashionable. I speak of cross-examination proper, and not the mere process of bringing before the court facts which either destroy the evidence of the witness or attack his credibility. The simple process of telling the jury that the witness is an anti-vaccinationist, or has made a written statement directly contrary to his testimony, or that he is separated from his wife, does not become cross-examination merely because it is put in the form of a question. Nor is it, I think, cross-examination to ask him two questions at once, or even to tell him the answers ; or to read to him the proofs of the witnesses who are about to be called on the other side, or to invite him to contradict the statements of those who have been called before him, or to repeat the evidence he has already given adverse to his cross-examiner. Some very successful advocates are in the habit of prefacing every other question with a *résumé* of their whole case, in a sort of ablative absolute ; but this is most usually done when the question does not require an answer, or is by its nature incapable of receiving one—as the most effective questions indeed generally are. To make speeches to the witness, instead of to the jury, is another device greatly in favour at the present day ; but it does not become cross-examination because it is done when the orator ought to be cross-examining. The beginner will usually find it easier to cross-examine his own witnesses, rather than those of his opponent, a method which was adopted with great success by Mr. Skimpin, junior counsel for the plaintiff in *Bardell v. Pickwick*. It will be remembered that in that *cause célèbre* Mr. Winkle was cross-examined with much severity when he ought to have been examined in chief; but the young advocate of to-day will be well advised only to proceed in this fashion when the witness is failing to come up to his proof. If he attempts it under any other circumstances, he ought at any rate to be quite sure of his judge. Mr. Justice Stareleigh has left no successors upon the Bench of the present day.

I have endeavoured to state (I hope not inaccurately) what cross-examination is not. If I am asked by captious critics to explain what it is, I can only answer, with humility and truthfulness, that I do not know. I once heard Serjeant Ballantine, when defending a prisoner at a small borough sessions, ask a witness how he spelt his name. With that question and answer the cross-examination began and ended, but only a master of the art is capable of so making bricks without straw.

.   .   .   .   .   .

There stands in the market-place of one of our Wessex towns a memorial cross—not, indeed, ancient, and scarcely beautiful, but bearing an inscription which is still read at assize time with wonder and rustic awe. It tells how one Ruth Pierce, of Potterne. did in the year 1753 combine with three others to buy a sack of wheat, each contributing her share of the price. When the money was collected a deficiency appeared, and each woman protested that she had paid her full share, Ruth, in particular, declaring that if she spoke untruly she wished that God might strike her dead. Thereupon it is recorded that she instantly fell lifeless to the ground, and the money was found hidden in her right hand. The inscription adds that this signal judgment of the Almighty was commemorated by the direction of the Mayor and Aldermen for the instruction of posterity.

It is probable, if not certain, that the event thus recorded actually happened; nor do I presume to doubt that it happened in accordance with that Divine omniscience and omnipotence, without which we are taught that not even a sparrow falls. Yet when we reflect how many liars have used the same blasphemous invocation with what seems to us impunity, and, at any rate, without the same immediate and awful retribution, it is difficult to resist a suspicion that some light upon the death of this poor Wiltshire cheat might have been derived from a post-mortem examination. We are reminded vaguely of those eighteen upon whom the tower in Siloam fell. The ancient sceptic, who was shown the votive tablets of grateful mariners hanging in the temple at Cythera, asked significantly in what shrine were preserved the offerings of the drowned. So have I, when passing from the market cross of Devizes to the Assize Courts hard by, reflected how much more easily justice would be administered if all perjury were cut as short as that of ill-fated Ruth.

Most men have learned—even without going circuit—that articulate speech, as a means of communicating ideas, is at best an imperfect makeshift. It is a degree better than the language of signs; and we believe it —on very slender grounds—to be several degrees superior to the thought transmission of insects or of birds. But it is quite inadequate to express anything so elusive and so impalpable as Truth. The formula has yet to be invented by which one human being can convey to another the certain knowledge that he is not lying. The ear has yet to be created which can detect the dissonance of Falsehood.

No doubt there are other reasons why civilization, in its despair, has recourse to courts of law; but this, after all, is the primary one. The whole machinery of justice, from the Lord Chancellor down to the humble barrister, the sage refinements of the law of evidence, the art of the advocate, and the wise discernment of the jury, are all devoted to the end of making the invisible seen, the inaudible heard, and the Truth known. Much has been done of late to soothe the consciences of witnesses, who may now asseverate in many forms and varied attitudes, after being tempted for a while with antiseptic Testaments in celluloid bindings to swear as did their fathers. But the ministers of the law may be profitably reminded that all their incantations are but necromancy after all, and may by ill-hap but half materialize the fair vision of Truth.

L'ENVOI

The dust of seventy circuits past,
   On ways well worn by frail humanity—
And shall the traveller at last
   Say naught, except that all was vanity?

From London town, a jovial crew
   We travelled all the Western Counties;
Nor recked we much when fees were few,
   And clients chary of their bounties.

How many miles of iron rail!
   How many briefs, in many places!
What sturdy struggles to prevail!
   And O! how many vanished faces!

Voices of once familiar tone,
   That often cheered my poor endeavour,
Footsteps that sounded by my own,
   Are silent now, and hushed for ever.

Through Taunton's meads, by Avon's tide,
   On Cornish moors, we strolled and jested;
And if with Fate dissatisfied,
   It was but seldom we confessed it.

The Table Round in Winton's hall,
   Fair Dorchester and bleak Devizes,
The front of Wells—I see them all,
   When still in dreams I go assizes.

So here to all who shared the strife
   By towers of Exe or spire of Sarum,
I pledge, in hope of larger life,
   The Circuit toast—" Cras Animarum! "

WILLIAM BRENDON AND SON, LTD.
PRINTERS, PLYMOUTH